Drug Maintenance Strategies in Schizophrenia

CLINICAL INSIGHTS

Drug Maintenance Strategies in Schizophrenia

Edited by
JOHN M. KANE, M.D.

Director, Psychiatric Research,
Long Island Jewish–Hillside Medical Center; and
Associate Professor of Psychiatry,
School of Medicine, Health Sciences Center,
State University of New York at Stony Brook

AMERICAN PSYCHIATRIC PRESS, INC.
Washington, D.C.

Library of Congress Cataloging in Publication Data

Main entry under title:

Drug maintenance strategies in schizophrenia.

(Clinical insights)
Includes bibliographies.
1. Schizophrenia—Chemotherapy. I. Kane, John M., 1945–
II. Series. [DNLM: 1. Schizophrenia—drug therapy. 2. Tranquilizing Agents, Major—adverse effects. 3. Tranquilizing Agents, Major—administration & dosage. WM 203 D794]
RC513.D73 1984 616.89'82061 84-14628
ISBN 0-88048-054-8 (pbk.)

Printed in the U.S.A.

Contents

Contributors

WILLIAM T. CARPENTER, JR., M.D.
Director, Maryland Psychiatric Research Center; and Professor of Psychiatry, University of Maryland School of Medicine, Baltimore

GARY FALTICO, Ph.D.
Veterans Administration Medical Center, West Los Angeles; and Brentwood Division and the Department of Psychiatry and Biobehavioral Sciences, University of California at Los Angeles

DOUGLAS W. HEINRICHS, M.D.
Chief, Outpatient Research Programs, Maryland Psychiatric Research Center; and Assistant Professor Psychiatry, University of Maryland School of Medicine, Baltimore

MARVIN I. HERZ, M.D.
Professor and Chairman, Department of Psychiatry, School of Medicine, State University of New York at Buffalo

JOHN M. KANE, M.D.
Director, Psychiatric Research, Long Island Jewish-Hillside Medical Center, Glen Oaks, New York; and Associate Professor of Psychiatry, School of Medicine, Health Sciences Center, State University of New York at Stony Brook

MALCA LEBELL, Ph.D.
Veterans Administration Medical Center, West Los Angeles; and Brentwood Division and the Department of Psychiatry and Biobehavioral Sciences, University of California at Los Angeles

STEPHEN R. MARDER, M.D.
Veterans Administration Medical Center, West Los Angeles; and Brentwood Division and the Department of Psychiatry and Biobehavioral Sciences, University of California at Los Angeles

JOANNE MCKENZIE, R.N.
Veterans Administration Medical Center, West Los Angeles; and Brentwood Division and the Department of Psychiatry and Biobehavioral Sciences, University of California at Los Angeles

JIM MINTZ, Ph.D.
Veterans Administration Medical Center, West Los Angeles; and Brentwood Division and the Department of Psychiatry and Biobehavioral Sciences, University of California at Los Angeles

ARTHUR RIFKIN, M.D.
Director, Division of Clinical Psychopharmacology Research, The Mount Sinai Medical Center; and Associate Professor of Psychiatry, The Mount Sinai School of Medicine, New York

NINA R. SCHOOLER, Ph.D.
National Institute of Mental Health, National Institutes of Health, Rockville, Maryland

THEODORE VAN PUTTEN, M.D.
Veterans Administration Medical Center, West Los Angeles; and Brentwood Division and the Department of Psychiatry and Biobehavioral Sciences, University of California at Los Angeles

Introduction

The efficacy of antipsychotic medication in the acute and long-term treatment of schizophrenia has been well established. Numerous double-blind placebo-controlled trials have demonstrated the value of drug treatment in alleviating the signs and symptoms of schizophrenia (Klein and Davis 1969) as well as reducing the risk of exacerbation or recurrence (Davis 1975). Although antipsychotic drugs may rival the effectiveness of accepted medications used in the treatment of medical disorders in other specialties, these medications have both limitations and risks.

The occurrence of tardive dyskinesia has become a major concern in the long-term utilization of antipsychotic medication. Several major reviews (Baldessarini et al. 1980; Fann et al. 1980; Jeste and Wyatt 1982; Kane and Smith 1982) have suggested the prevalence of tardive dyskinesia to be approximately 15 percent. The prevalence clearly varies, however, depending on the population studied. Rates as high as 50 to 60 percent have been reported among chronically institutionalized individuals (Kane and Smith 1982). Although the majority of patients developing this condition experience relatively mild and apparently nonprogressive signs and symptoms (Casey 1983; Gardos et al. 1983; Kane et al. 1983), some individuals do develop a severe and potentially very disabling form of the disorder. At present, we are unable to identify those patients most at risk for the more severe or persistent types of tardive dyskinesia.

Incidence figures from an ongoing prospective study of tardive dyskinesia development suggest an incidence of 3 to 4 percent per year of neuroleptic exposure, at least for the first 4 to 5 years of treatment (Kane et al. 1982).

Antipsychotic drugs are clearly implicated as the single most important etiologic factor in the development of abnormal involuntary movements among patients receiving these compounds, although the evidence is largely epidemiologic. Dosage and duration of drug administration have generally been assumed to be major risk factors in the development of tardive dyskinesia. The data available, however, are not convincing in supporting this assumption except in a few studies that focused largely on patients relatively early in their treatment history (Kane and Smith 1982). It may be that this is the phase in treatment when the introduction of alternative long-term pharmacotherapeutic strategies will have its greatest impact. A great deal of work will be necessary, however, to establish clear-cut guidelines. This issue has served as a major impetus for exploring new approaches.

Other factors supporting the need for these investigations include the occurrence of clinically significant extrapyramidal side effects, even among patients who have received antipsychotic medication on a long-term basis (Rifkin et al. 1978). At times, these adverse effects may be subtle or may be mistaken for psychopathological phenomena, such as anxiety or depression.

In addition, some investigators have suggested that antipsychotic medication may produce states of subjective dysphoria or lack of motivation unrelated to extrapyramidal effects. Although further work is needed to elucidate what role drugs may play in these phenomena (which are frequent manifestations of the illness itself), this too has stimulated further evaluation of the benefit-to-risk ratio of neuroleptic treatment.

The presumed heterogeneity of schizophrenia has also highlighted the need for further research as to indications for and benefits from long-term pharmacologic treatment. Although the majority of well-diagnosed multi-episode schizophrenic patients relapse following withdrawal from medication, there are some who remain well for substantial periods of time. On the other hand, there are patients who relapse despite continued administration of medication (even when compliance is assured by the use of long-acting injectable medications).

The problem we face as clinicians is making long-term treatment recommendations for a given patient without the availability of clinical predictors. Despite numerous attempts, we do not have established indicators of how patients will fare with or without antipsychotic medication. As clinicians, we develop some intuition or clinical sense as to what strategy is best suited for a given patient. It can be very difficult, however, to make judgments regarding probable cause and effect with small numbers of patients and without the appropriate controls.

During the same period that the psychiatric field has developed extensive knowledge regarding antipsychotic drugs, considerable advances have been made in the design and methodology employed in clinical trials. As mental health professionals, we are keenly aware of the need for objectivity, elimination of bias, and avoidance of premature closure on a given issue. The development of specific diagnostic criteria, double-blind random assignment design, standardized assessment measures, and so on have been attempts to improve the likelihood of our finding meaningful and reproducible differences between treatments. Despite the increasing sophistication of both our methods and the statistical interpretation of our results, clinical trials remain extremely difficult and expensive to carry out, and the development of new strategies seems painfully slow at times.

In recent years, advances have been made in improving the reliability and validity of diagnostic criteria. In addition, more comprehensive assessment measures have been developed to follow not only the psychopathological signs and symptoms characteristic of schizophrenia, but also levels of social and vocational adjustment, family interactions, mood disorders, and a variety of adverse effects.

In providing an introduction to the strategies described in this monograph, it is also important to review the conceptual basis for the long-term treatment of schizophrenia. We generally divide treatment into three phases, which cannot necessarily be clearly delineated in any given patient. The acute treatment phase is that in which a new episode or a substantial exacerbation of preexisting symptoms is treated. The response to this phase of treatment will, to some extent, determine the rationale and expectations for subsequent treatment. If a patient fully recovers or improves substantially, the continuation phase of treatment begins at the point of maximum improvement. This point may occur after weeks or even months. The assumption underlying continuation treatment is that, in an illness with remissions and exacerbations, an episode that goes untreated might have a finite length. (This model is perhaps more obviously relevant to affective illness, but would also play a role in thinking about some schizophrenic patients as well.) The drug treatment that alleviates the signs and symptoms of an acute episode appears to be necessary to maintain that improvement for a period of time at least as long as the episode would have lasted had it gone untreated. Once this period has passed, a recurrence of symptoms could be considered a "new episode" rather than a reemergence of the original episode. The point at which continuation treatment ends is the point at which true preventive or prophylactic treatment begins, the goal of which is the prevention of a new episode.

There are many patients for whom this model may not apply. A substantial proportion of schizophrenic patients remain continuously symptomatic despite vigorous pharmacotherapy. Some of these patients would be far worse without medication, and pharmacotherapy could be viewed as controlling existing psychotic symptomatology to some extent. Clearly, these patients may be poor candidates for drug withdrawal or substantial dosage reduction.

Much of this remains theoretical. The time involved in different phases of the illness is likely to vary from individual to individual and, in all likelihood, may depend on the phase of illness (in a larger sense) that a given patient is in. Despite this likely heterogeneity, a review of the literature (Kane et al. in press) does suggest that this conceptual framework may have some practical significance. Those maintenance medication studies focusing on patients recently discharged from the hospital following recovery (or partial recovery) from an acute exacerbation or acute episode have reported substantially higher relapse rates for patients receiving medication (Hogarty et al. 1979; Schooler et al. 1980), than those studies focusing on patients who had been in remission or at a stable clinical plateau in the community for several months or longer (Rifkin et al. 1977; Quitkin et al. 1978; Kane et al. 1983). The efficacy of different maintenance strategies may be determined to some extent by the phase of illness.

Another factor in determining the benefits of these strategies is the outcome criteria utilized. Investigators vary in the way in which they define relapse or failure on a given treatment. In addition, these strategies to some extent depend upon an early recognition of approaching relapse so that dosage can be increased or medication can be reinstituted to forestall a full-blown psychotic episode. The identification of so-called prodromal signs and symptoms remains a critical problem in this context. Since many schizophrenic patients experience periods of increasing nonpsychotic symptomatology (e.g., depression, anxiety, obsessive thoughts) that do not necessarily represent prodromata of a psychotic episode, the reliability and validity of our judgments regarding imminent relapse must be studied and not taken for granted.

These and a variety of other issues will come into better focus as specific examples of alternative treatment strategies are presented. This monograph provides an overview of much of the major research being conducted in this area. It is important to point out that as yet these strategies have not been directly compared with one another. Now that some evidence has accumulated regarding their feasibility, this is clearly the next step.

John M. Kane, M.D.

References

Baldessarini RJ, Cole JO, Davis JM, et al: Tardive dyskinesia (Task Force Report no. 18). Washington, DC, American Psychiatric Association, 1980

Casey DE: Tardive dyskinesia: what is the natural history? International Drug Therapy Newsletter 18:13–16, 1983

Davis J: Overview: maintenance therapy in psychiatry, I. schizophrenia. Am J Psychiatry 132:1237–1245, 1975

Fann WE, Smith RC, Davis JM, et al (eds): Tardive Dyskinesia: Research and Treatment. New York, Spectrum Publications, 1980

Gardos B, Perenyi A, Cole JO: Tardive dyskinesia: changes after 3 years. J Clin Psychopharmacol 3:315–318, 1983

Hogarty G, Schooler NR, Uhlrich R, et al: Fluphenazine in social therapy in the aftercare of schizophrenic patients. Arch Gen Psychiatry 36:1283–1294, 1979

Jeste DV, Wyatt RJ: Understanding and Treating Tardive Dyskinesia. New York, Guilford Press, 1982

Kane JM, Smith JM: Tardive dyskinesia: prevalence and risk factors, 1959–1979. Arch Gen Psychiatry 39:473–481, 1982

Kane JM, Woerner M, Weinhold P, et al.: A prospective study of tardive dyskinesia development: preliminary results. J Clin Psychopharmacol 2:345–349, 1982

Kane JM, Rifkin A, Woerner M, et al: Low dose neuroleptic treatment of outpatient schizophrenics; I: preliminary results for relapse rates. Arch Gen Psychiatry 40:893–896, 1983

Kane JM, Lieberman J, Moeglin J-M: Maintenance drug treatment in schizophrenia: a review, in Progress in Psychiatric Drug Treatment, Vol. 3. Edited by Klein DF, Kane JM. Littleton, John Wright-PSG (in press)

Klein DF, Davis JM: Diagnosis and Drug Treatment of Psychiatric Disorders. Baltimore, Williams & Wilkins Co, 1969

Quitkin F, Rifkin A, Kane JM, et al: Long-acting oral versus injectable antipsychotic drugs in schizophrenia. Arch Gen Psychiatry 35:889–892, 1978

Rifkin A, Quitkin F, Rabiner CJ, et al: Fluphenazine decanoate, fluphenazine hydrochloride given orally, and placebo in remitted schizophrenics; I: relapse rates after one year. Arch Gen Psychiatry 34:43–47, 1977

Rifkin A, Quitkin F, Kane JM, et al: Are prophylactic antiparkinson drugs necessary? A controlled study of procyclidine withdrawal. Arch Gen Psychiatry 35:483–489, 1978

Schooler NR, Levine J, Severe JV, et al: Prevention of relapse in schizophrenia: an evaluation on fluphenazine decanoate. Arch Gen Psychiatry 37:16–24, 1980

1

Dosage Reduction Strategies in the Long-Term Treatment of Schizophrenia

John M. Kane, M.D.

1

Dosage Reduction Strategies in the Long-Term Treatment of Schizophrenia

The efficacy of long-term antipsychotic drug treatment in reducing psychotic relapse among schizophrenics has been well established (Davis 1975). Despite variations in patient characteristics and methodology the overwhelming majority of controlled, long-term studies demonstrate a clinically and statistically significant advantage for drug over placebo in preventing psychotic relapse and rehospitalization. This appears to be the case even following recovery from an acute onset, first episode of schizophrenic illness (Kane et al. 1982).

Very little work has been done, however, in attempting to identify minimum effective medication dosage levels for long-term treatment. The desire to reduce adverse effects, particularly tardive dyskinesia, has led to increasing interest in this problem.

The dosage reduction strategy assumes to some extent that continuous medication, even in low doses, is preferable to intermittent treatment. The suggestion has been made that relapses occurring in patients already receiving some medication may be less severe or may respond more rapidly than those occurring in untreated patients. Others have suggested that patient compliance and acceptance of the need for continued treatment may benefit from ongoing pharmacotherapy. In addition, the intuitive notion that discontinuous treatment might reduce the incidence, severity, or persistence of tardive dyskinesia requires clinical testing. All of these possibilities are hypotheses to be tested, and future studies should involve more direct comparisons of different strategies.

METHODOLOGICAL ISSUES

Attempts to identify minimal dose requirements have taken three major paths: (1) examining the relationship between dosage and relapse in those reported clinical trials that allow such analysis; (2) conducting prospective studies comparing patients undergoing gradual dosage reduction to controls maintained on stable dose; and (3) assigning comparisons of different fixed dose levels randomly.

The first type of analysis is complicated by the fact that dosage may have been influenced by a variety of factors and cannot be assumed to be random. Dosage manipulations may not have been carried out in a systematic, objective, reproducible fashion. In the second type of study, dosage reduction and time may be confounded. Even if patients are discontinued from medication completely, a relapse may not occur for several weeks or months. In a gradual dosage reduction strategy, it would be difficult to determine minimum effective dosage given the unpredictable time frame in which patients relapse. The third strategy eliminates some of the concerns raised above. However, a fixed dose or dose range must be set, and this has generally been somewhat arbitrary given the lack of available data. This design does not necessarily identify a minimum dose for a given individual, although it does provide some guidelines as to where to begin.

Baldessarini and Davis (1980) reviewed those controlled studies that permitted estimates of the equivalent dose of chlorpromazine to be plotted against reduction of relapse. They found no significant dosage effect from 100 to 2,000 mg/day or more (median, 310 mg/day) and no mean difference in outcome at dosages above versus below 310 mg/day. They also considered that differences in patient populations and treatment settings may have complicated attempts to find dosage effects on relapse rates. Therefore, they examined the correlation between relapse rate on placebo (which they suggested could be used as an indicator of illness severity) and mean dose of medication to which the drug-treated group had been assigned. Their inability to find a significant correlation suggested that those patients who were more ill (or at greater risk of relapsing after discontinuation of drug use) were not necessarily treated with higher doses of medication.

GRADUAL DOSE REDUCTION STUDIES

Greenberg and Roth (1966) studied 42 male inpatients (mean age, 42) who had been receiving the same dose of chlorpromazine (mean, 510 mg/day) for a minimum of 8 months. All patients had been clinically stable for at least 6 months. The patients were randomly assigned double-blind either to continue their medication as before or to have an additional day of placebo substituted for active medication each 8 weeks. When after 60 weeks the experimental group began to receive placebo only, the control group was abruptly withdrawn from chlorpromazine and placed on placebo.

Greenberg and Roth did not find any significant difference between the two groups during the experimental period (prior to the complete termination of chlorpromazine in both groups), suggesting that the patients undergoing gradual dosage reduction were able to maintain their clinical stability. Both groups showed a significant deterioration in their clinical ratings after total withdrawal of chlorpromazine. The authors concluded that lower maintenance dosages could be utilized in these patients.

Branchey et al. (1981) studied 32 inpatients (mean age, 51) who had been chronically hospitalized (mean duration, 25 years). All patients had been treated with neuroleptics for at least 5 years and received the same drug dose for at least 3 months. Before beginning the study, the neuroleptics the patients were taking were replaced by equivalent doses of loxapine in liquid form. Patients were randomly assigned to two groups double-blind.

Twenty-one patients were assigned to the experimental group in which drug dose was decreased according to a predetermined schedule in successive steps of 4 weeks' duration—to one-half, one-fourth, and one-eighth of its initial value. This was followed by placebo substitution for 24 weeks. Eleven control patients were maintained on the same amount of loxapine throughout the study. At baseline, the experimental group received a mean ± SD daily dose of loxapine of 71 ± 45 mg; the controls received 66 ± 44 mg. Level of psychopathology was assessed at 2-week intervals.

Of the 21 patients whose medication was decreased and then discontinued, 16 (76 percent) relapsed in contrast to 2 (18 percent) of the controls. Only one patient relapsed during the period of progressive drug reduction. The interval between drug discontinuation and relapse for the other 15 patients varied from 2 to 14 weeks. The mean daily dose of loxapine given at the end of the baseline period was lower in the patients who did not relapse (40 ± 7) than in those who relapsed (81 ± 50). Baseline Brief Psychiatric Rating Scale scores were similar in nonrelapsing patients (37 ± 5) and in relapsing patients (37 ± 7).

In effect, 20 of the 21 patients undergoing a gradual drug reduction to one-eighth of the initial dose carried out over a 3-month period did not show signs of deterioration. This could be interpreted as suggesting that these patients could have been maintained on doses of neuroleptics much lower than those they were routinely receiving. It could also suggest that the deterioration resulting from substantial dosage reduction does not occur immediately. Many patients discontinued abruptly from neuroleptics do not relapse immediately, and the majority of patients in relative remission do not relapse for the first 3 months (Hogarty and Uhlrich 1977). Age, baseline level of psychopathology, baseline dosage of medication, and other factors might be related to relapse rates and time course of relapse in such a study.

The major concern is separating the effects of time and dosage reduction. Interestingly, it was anticipated that patients would recover when treated with medication doses that had been effective in preventing relapse during the drug reduction period. This turned out not to be the case. Most patients needed a much higher dose. In fact, 8 of 13 patients required a dose equivalent to or higher than that used before the start of the study. This highlights the importance of considering treatment response of a new episode or relapse as one important outcome measure in studying various long-term treatment strategies.

FIXED DOSE COMPARISONS

Few studies have attempted to assess prospectively the efficacy of different fixed doses or dosage ranges in preventing relapse.

Caffey et al. (1964) studied 348 men under the age of 56 who had been hospitalized for 2 or more years. They had been treated with fairly stable doses of 100 to 800 mg/day (mean, 350–400) of either chlorpromazine or thioridazine for at least 3 months prior to beginning the study.

Patients were randomly assigned to one of four groups. One group continued to receive either chlorpromazine or thioridazine daily at their established dosage. A second group received a reduced total dosage on an intermittent schedule; specifically, they received their usual daily dose on Monday, Wednesday, and Friday only. There was a corresponding placebo group for both of the two medication groups. Patients were continued double-blind for 16 weeks or until they showed a definite change for the worse and, in the judgment of the attending physician, should be returned to known medication. By the end of 4 months, 5 percent of the patients continued on their usual dose had relapsed, as did 15 percent of those on the three-sevenths dose. In comparison, 45 percent of the placebo-treated patients relapsed. All three percentages are significantly different from one another.

For a 6-week period, Goldstein et al. (1978) studied the efficacy of two dose levels of fluphenazine enanthate, with and without crisis-oriented family therapy, in 104 recently discharged, schizophrenic patients. These predominantly (69 percent) first episode schizophrenics (mean age, 23 ± 4.2) were randomly assigned to fluphenazine enanthate 1 ml (25 mg) or 0.25 ml (6.25 mg) following hospital admission. During the hospitalization (mean stay, 14 days), additional oral phenothiazines could be given. Following discharge, patients received only fluphenazine enanthate injections every other week for the 6-week outpatient phase. Patients were stratified according to premorbid adjustment prior to random assignment to one of the four treatment groups. Relapse was defined as the need to alter medication substantially or to rehospitalize the patient. Only 10 percent relapsed within the

6 weeks following discharge, but 24 percent of those in the low dose, no-therapy condition relapsed as compared to none of the high dose, therapy group. The low dose, therapy and the high dose, no-therapy groups had relapse rates of 9 percent and 10 percent, respectively. Although this study involved a relatively brief period of controlled treatment, the results suggest the potential interaction between dosage and such psychotherapeutic interventions as crisis-oriented family therapy.

My colleagues and I (Kane et al. 1979, 1983) have conducted a series of studies employing low dose fluphenazine—1.25–5.0 mg biweekly—representing one-tenth of the standard 12.5–50 mg biweekly used in previous maintenance medication studies at the same institution (Rifkin et al. 1977; Quitkin et al. 1978). To test the efficacy of this dosage range, three separate experiments were carried out: (1) an open trial in 57 patients, lasting 6 months; (2) a double-blind, placebo-controlled, discontinuation study in a subgroup of patients who maintained good remission throughout the entire 6-month open trial; and (3) a double-blind comparison of low dose and standard dose fluphenazine decanoate involving 126 patients.

Study 1

The 57 patients (39 men) participating in the open trial met the following criteria: (1) having a probable or definite schizophrenia, any subtype (except acute first episode), according to the Research Diagnostic Criteria (Spitzer et al. 1977); (2) experiencing a remission for at least 4 weeks or at a stable clinical plateau despite vigorous chemotherapy; (3) not requiring adjunctive pharmacotherapy other than antiparkinsonian agents or occasional benzodiazepines; (4) being free of clinically significant side effects; and (5) receiving standard doses of fluphenazine decanoate. The patients had a mean age 27.2 ± 6.4 years. They had had 2.4 ± 1.3 previous episodes and had been in remission for 12.5 ± 12.3 months. Age at onset of illness was 21.2 ± 6.4.

Patients were openly switched to a dilute preparation of fluphenazine decanoate (2.5 mg/ml) specially prepared for use in this study. The starting dose of the dilute preparation was determined by baseline dosage of standard fluphenazine. Relapse was defined as any increase in or reemergence of significant symptoms suggesting imminent psychotic relapse. Patients were seen biweekly by the research psychiatrist.

Eight patients dropped out of the study after 9.6 ± 7 weeks (range 2–26) without evidence of clinical deterioration. One patient manifested abnormal involuntary movements following dosage reduction and was removed from the study. Fifteen patients relapsed after 16.7 ± 6.2 weeks (range 6–26). The cumulative proportion of patients relapsing by the end of 6 months was 30 percent (95 percent confidence interval of 17–43 percent).

Only one of the 15 patients who relapsed required rehospitalization; 12 recovered within 1 month of dosage increase. This suggested that the low dose treatment might be a viable strategy for maintaining patients in the community while keeping total cumulative dose to a minimum.

In an open, uncontrolled pilot study, it was not possible to determine whether the patients successfully treated with minimal doses were patients benefiting from the medication or patients who would have maintained remission without drug treatment.

Study 2

A double-blind, discontinuation study was carried out in 16 patients who completed 6 months of open, low dose treatment without any signs of clinical deterioration. Patients were matched for age, sex, age of onset of illness, and length of remission. One member of each pair was randomly assigned to placebo and the other to active, low dose treatment. This design allowed for sequential analysis so that, if statistical significance were reached, no new patients would enter the study. Sequential analysis reached significance when five patients relapsed on placebo and one on active medication ($p<.04$, Spicer's closed plan; 1-sided alternative) (Spicer 1962). No new patients entered the study at that point. The ultimate outcome for those patients already entered was 7 of 8 placebo-treated patients relapsed at 18 ± 8.5

weeks (range 7–26). One patient on active drug relapsed at the 25th week. These results supported our conclusion that the low dose range utilized is clinically active. In addition, these findings would argue against the suggestion discussed previously that lack of relapse following drug withdrawal is related to the prewithdrawal medication dosage level.

Study 3

The results of the third study, a prospective double-blind comparison of low dose and standard dose fluphenazine, are reported in the next chapter.

CONCLUSION

The studies reviewed support the conclusion that a substantial proportion of patients may be maintained on lower doses of medication than are frequently employed on a long-term basis. At present, there are no established means of clinically predicting which patients are most likely to tolerate or benefit from substantial dosage reduction. Whether or not biological measures such as antipsychotic drug blood level, prolactin response, or response to a pharmacologic probe (Janowsky et al. 1973; Angrist et al. 1981; Lieberman et al. 1984) might be useful in this context remains to be established.

References

Angrist B, Peselow E, Rotrosen J, et al: Relationships between response to dopamine agonists, psychopathology, neuroleptic treatment response, and need for neuroleptic maintenance in schizophrenic subjects, in Recent Advances in Neuropsychopharmacology. Edited by Angrist B, Burrows G. New York, Pergamon Press, 1981, 49–54

Baldessarini RJ, Davis JM: What *is* the best maintenance dose of neuroleptics in schizophrenia? Psychiatry Res 3:115–122, 1980

Branchey MH, Branchey LB, Richardson MA: Effects of neuroleptic adjustment on clinical condition and tardive dyskinesia in schizophrenic patients. Am J Psychiatry 130:608–612, 1981

Caffey EM, Diamond LS, Frank TV, et al: Discontinuation or reduction of chemotherapy in chronic schizophrenia. J Chronic Dis 17:347–358, 1964

Davis JM: Overview: maintenance therapy in psychiatry: I: schizophrenia. Am J Psychiatry 132:1237–1245, 1975

Goldstein M, Rodnick E, Evans J, et al: Drug and family therapy in the aftercare treatment of schizophrenics. Arch Gen Psychiatry 35:1169–1177, 1978

Greenberg L, Roth S: Differential effect of abrupt vs gradual withdrawal of chlorpromazine in hospitalized chronic schizophrenic patients. Am J Psychiatry 123:221–226, 1966

Hogarty GE, Uhlrich RF: Temporal effects of drug and placebo in delaying relapse in schizophrenic outpatients. Arch Gen Psychiatry 34:297–301, 1977

Janowsky DS, Lel-Wousef K, Davis JM, et al: Provocation of schizophrenic symptoms by intravenous methylphenidate. Arch Gen Psychiatry 28:185–191, 1973

Kane JM, Rifkin A, Quitkin F, et al: Low dose fluphenazine decanoate in maintenance treatment in schizophrenia. Psychiatry Res 1:341–348, 1979

Kane JM, Quitkin F, Rifkin A, et al: Fluphenazine vs placebo in patients with remitted acute first episode schizophrenia. Arch Gen Psychiatry 39:70–73, 1982

Kane JM, Rifkin A, Woerner M, et al: Low dose neuroleptics in the treatment of outpatient schizophrenics; I: relapse rates preliminary results. Arch Gen Psychiatry 40:893–896, 1983

Lieberman JA, Kane JM, Gadaleta D, et al: Methylphenidate challenge as a predictor of relapse in schizophrenia. Am J Psychiatry 141:633–638, 1984

Quitkin F, Rifkin A, Kane JM, et al: Long-acting oral vs injectable antipsychotic drugs in schizophrenics. Arch Gen Psychiatry 35:889–892, 1978

Rifkin A, Quitkin F, Rabiner CJ, et al: Fluphenazine decanoate, fluphenazine hydrochloride given orally, and placebo in remitted schizophrenics; I: relapse rates after 1 year. Arch Gen Psychiatry 34:43–47, 1977

Spicer CC: Some new closed sequential design for clinical trials. Biometrics 18:203, 1962

Spitzer RL, Endicott J, Robins E: Research Diagnostic Criteria (RDC) for a Selected Group of Functional Disorders, 3rd ed. New York, New York State Psychiatric Institute, 1977

2

Low-Dose Neuroleptic Maintenance Treatment of Schizophrenia

Arthur Rifkin, M.D.
John M. Kane, M.D.

2

Low-Dose Neuroleptic Maintenance Treatment of Schizophrenia

This chapter describes and discusses a study of low-dose fluphenazine decanoate (FD) in the long-term treatment of schizophrenia. The rationale for such a study and a review of previous related studies have been presented in the previous chapter. The overall goal of this study was twofold: we wished to see whether low-dose FD affected the rate of relapse, and whether it affected social adjustment.

Any study of the long-term treatment of schizophrenia should specify carefully the stage of the disorder which is being treated. Results obtained with subjects who are in remission of psychotic symptoms may be quite different from results obtained with subjects who are not in remission. Subjects who have had a partial response to neuroleptics, but remained psychotic, may have a different response to long-term treatment with neuroleptics than that of subjects who have no or only mild psychotic symptoms. Most previous studies of long-term treatment have not specified what stage of remission the subjects are in. We have shown that when subjects with schizophrenia but no psychotic symptoms were entered into a placebo-controlled comparison of FD and oral fluphenazine, the relapse rate with both active drugs within 1 year was about 10 percent, a rate much lower than other similar studies that did not specify the degree of remission at entry (Rifkin et al.

1977). This suggests that degree of remission is related to vulnerability to relapse.

It should be noted that an alternative explanation is possible. In order to enter subjects who are in remission from psychotic symptoms into a long-term treatment study, it is necessary to have a period of time between discharge from inpatient treatment and entry into the study in order to treat those who are not in remission and to assess the stability of the remission. In our study (Rifkin et al. 1977), we waited at least 4 weeks after the subject entered remission before assigning the experimental treatment to be reasonably certain that the remission was stable.

This delay in entering patients means that such patients differ from those in the other studies not only by degree of remission but by interval from discharge. Both facts may be associated with vulnerability to relapse. Our conclusion that the relapse rate is lower in persons with schizophrenia in full remission compared to those in partial remission, when treated with standard doses of a neuroleptic, must be tempered by the possibility that the time elapsed since discharge may also be responsible.

Nevertheless, it seems important to take degree of remission into account in any comparison of treatments. In the present study, we examined subjects who were in full or nearly full remission of psychotic symptoms.

When someone with schizophrenia is admitted to or discharged from inpatient treatment, it is not purely according to severity of symptoms. Much depends on the stated or unstated attitudes of psychiatrists in the community, on the availability of inpatient facilities, on the pressure for these beds, on the attitude of third-party payers toward length of stay, and on other factors. The decision to admit or discharge someone with schizophrenia, therefore, should not be the prime determinant of whether the subject is considered to be responding to treatment.

We define remission and relapse by operational, objective criteria. Whether the subject is hospitalized during relapse is important information, but relapse is determined independently. There are disadvantages to defining relapse and remission in an objective operational fashion. In routine clinical practice, relapse is not determined by a score on a rating scale. It is determined by the clinician's global judgment, which varies from patient to patient, as it should, because the clinician uses information idiosyncratic to the individuals such as sequence of symptoms in previous relapses, severity and consequences of symptoms in previous relapses, and probably other factors that a sensitive clinician can respond to without necessarily being able to articulate clearly.

For example, we know a patient whose initial symptom of relapse is mild catatonic behavior, such as hesitating and briefly standing motionless before he enters or leaves his apartment. It is reasonable to alter his drug treatment when this behavior occurs and not wait for definite psychotic symptoms to appear. We used definite psychotic symptoms to define relapse and remission in this study because the idiosyncratic prodromal symptoms are not reliably known, nor can they be proven prodromal. The clinician may feel certain of connections between symptoms, but it is difficult to prove this with accepted standards of testing hypotheses. This is the strength and weakness of scientific standards of hypothesis testing—what it tests is rigorous, but much of what clinicians do does not conform to such standards. Studies in other chapters of this monograph used prodromal symptoms as the determinant in changing drug treatment. We chose in our study to be more certain of relapse before changing treatment and considering the patient to be relapsed. As with all studies using objective operational criteria, we sacrificed routine clinical practice for a more rigorous research technique to test our hypotheses. This increase in certainty is bought at the price of generalizability of our results to the clinician, who does not use our rating scales or our criteria to determine relapse. We believe the gains of our approach are greater than the drawbacks, but the reader should be aware of this problem in relating research findings to clinical practice.

The obvious question in comparing drug treatments of schizophrenia is the relapse rate. Less obvious is the question of whether social adjustment is affected by drug treatment. Psychiatrists tend to be concerned mainly with symptoms of psychopathology, both in arriving at diagnoses and in choosing treatments. We are less concerned, usually, with issues such as how the patient is alienating friends and coworkers, or the burden on the family of living with the patient. Yet such concerns may affect the lives of patients and their families as much as or more than psychopathological symptoms. A major goal of the present study was to assess social adjustment and to determine the influence of FD dosage. Dosage may affect relapse and social adjustment.

Concern over adverse reactions to neuroleptic medication has centered largely over symptoms that directly affect the body and are observable in the examining room and in laboratory tests, or are uncomfortable to the patient and reported to the physician. Information about social functioning is often missing. We use the term *social* here in a very broad context to mean all behavior with others, or the absence of expected or desired behavior. This includes behavior at home with the family, with acquaintances, at work, and, especially with persons who have schizophrenia and usually do not attain sufficient vocational competence to achieve paid employment, at volunteer jobs or rehabilitation programs.

We think it is important to focus not only on the patient's behavior but also its impact on the family. Patients may not be aware of the effect of their behavior and may not, when questioned, report difficulties. Family members may have quite a different story to tell. A patient's behavior may be quite burdensome and, like a stone thrown into a quiet lake, may produce ripples of painful effects on those who live with the patient or who are more indirectly affected, for example, the employer of the patient's father.

For too long we have focused narrowly on the patient's symptoms to the neglect of these wider effects. In this study, we took great pains to determine these effects. We would like to acknowledge the assistance of two individuals who have played the major role in developing and evaluating the rating scale used to measure social adjustment: Delores Kreisman, Ph.D., and Richard Blumenthal, Ph.D., both of New York State Psychiatric Institute in New York City.

SUBJECTS

The subjects were selected from psychiatric outpatient clinics at three institutions. These institutions vary in the type of patient who uses their facilities. At the first, Long Island Jewish–Hillside Medical Center, most patients are white middle-income persons. The second, New York State Psychiatric Institute, is situated in a poor, largely black neighborhood; the subjects come from an outpatient clinic which serves a catchment area in that neighborhood. The third, Mount Sinai Medical Clinic, is a private, voluntary, nonprofit hospital on the border of Spanish Harlem (a poor Hispanic community) and the upper east side of Manhattan (a largely white middle-class neighborhood). The psychiatric clinic does not serve a catchment area. Patients come to the hospital from a wide area of metropolitan New York City.

Consequently, the ethnic and socioeconomic mix of subjects in this study is varied. The proportion of black participants, for example, is significantly greater at New York State Psychiatric Institute than at the other sites. We hope that this diversity increases the generalizability of our findings.

Subjects were between the ages of 17 and 60 years. All, during their most severe periods, met criteria for schizophrenia or schizoaffective disorder using the Research Diagnostic Criteria (Spitzer et al. 1977). We excluded patients with tardive dyskinesia, serious drug abuse, alcoholism, or physical illness, and those requiring any adjunctive psychotropic medicine other than antianxiety or antiparkinsonian agents. All subjects gave informed consent. This study was approved by the institutional review boards of each of the institutions involved.

METHODOLOGY

Overall Design

The overall design of this project was to assess the effect of a very low dose of FD, in comparison to standard doses, on relapse and on social adjustment. A secondary question was to determine whether there were important differences in adverse reactions, especially dyskinetic symptoms. This was considered secondary because we doubted our sample would be large enough to demonstrate a difference in dyskinetic symptoms during 12 months. A very large difference would be required.

Most studies of long-term drug treatment of schizophrenia have used the interval to relapse as the main outcome measure. Not wishing to confine ourselves to this, we tried to determine whether the treatments in question affected multiple relapses. Therefore, a subject who relapsed was not removed from the study. Instead, the experimental medication was continued and "open" adjunctive neuroleptic medication was given, while the subject was either continued in outpatient treatment or transferred to inpatient care. Once the psychotic symptoms remitted, the subject was gradually removed from the adjunctive neuroleptic and continued on the experimental drug alone. In this fashion, we could assess the effect of these treatments on the incidence of multiple relapses. After two relapses, we had to withdraw a subject from the study. Some subjects chose not to remain in the study after a relapse, so we were not able to follow all subjects through relapses.

Potential subjects were selected from the inpatient and outpatient services of the three institutions, and the courses of their disorders were followed to determine eligibility. To be eligible, the subject had to meet our criteria for remission for at least 4 weeks. During this 4-week period, the potential subject had to maintain clinical stability as determined by absence of fluctuation on the Global Assessment Scale (GAS) (Spitzer et al. 1976) of more than 10 points or one point on any of four items of the Brief Psychiatric Rating Scale (BPRS) (Overall and Gorham 1962), which assessed psychotic symptoms of conceptual disorganization, hallucinatory behavior, suspiciousness, and unusual thought content.

During this preliminary phase, all potential subjects were treated with FD as their only neuroleptic, which usually required a switch from the drug with which they were being treated. The 4 weeks of clinical stability had to occur during treatment with FD. If this stability could not be achieved within a dose range of 0.5 to

2.0 ml (12.5 to 50 mg) every 2 weeks because of lack of therapeutic efficacy or adverse reactions, the potential subject was considered ineligible.

If a potential subject was not in complete remission from all psychotic symptoms during this preliminary phase, an effort was made to achieve complete remission by a higher dose of neuroleptic—either FD or some other. If this failed to bring the patient to full remission, we reduced the dose and used FD within the limits described, and accepted the patient into the study if our criteria for remission were met, as will be described.

Psychosocial Treatment

No attempt was made to control for psychosocial treatment. All three institutions offered psychotherapy and rehabilitative services, although these were not offered to all subjects. We believe the type and extent of psychosocial treatment given to these subjects was representative of what is given to similar patients in reasonably staffed mental health clinics.

Medication

The manufacturer of FD prepared for our use a 10-times dilution that had the identical appearance to regular FD. In most instances, the treating psychiatrist administered the injection from a specially labelled vial in a manner to maintain the double-blind condition. For the initial dose at entry into the study, i.e., at the point of randomization to one of the dosages, the volume of injection that had been used during the stabilization period was given. For example, if the subject received 1.0 ml every 2 weeks during the stabilization period, which lasted at least 4 weeks, then 1.0 ml of study medication was given at entry into the study, which would contain 25 mg or 2.5 mg of FD, depending on which dilution was used. Study injections were given every 2 weeks. The treating psychiatrist could change the dose within the range of 0.5 to 2.0 ml every 2 weeks, according to the subject's clinical condition. The psychiatrist was urged to use the lowest dose that kept the subject at least as free of psychotic symptoms as at baseline.

Benztropine was given as needed if extrapyramidal symptoms emerged. If insomnia was a persistent problem that bothered the subject, the treating psychiatrist was permitted to administer a benzodiazepine at night.

If the subject relapsed (see below for definition), the treating psychiatrist gave adjunctive "open" neuroleptic medication while continuing the biweekly injections of study FD, and discontinued the adjunctive neuroleptic on remission. If the subject could not be treated in the clinic during the relapse and required hospitalization, an effort was made to continue the study FD during hospitalization while the subject received an adjunctive neuroleptic. If this was not possible, study FD was resumed when the subject returned to the clinic.

Measures

Three sets of measures were completed by the treating psychiatrist. The first, the BPRS, is an 18-item scale covering the full range of psychotic symptoms. This was completed monthly. The second set included a record of dosage, adverse reactions, and the Clinical Global Impression Scale (CGI) (Guy 1976). The CGI is a 7-point scale divided into two parts. One part measures degree of severity; the other, degree of change from baseline.

At 12-week intervals, three additional scales were completed: (1) the Simpson Dyskinesia Scale (Simpson et al. 1979), a measure of abnormal involuntary movements used in reaching a diagnosis of tardive dyskinesia; (2) the Simpson-Angus Scale (Simpson and Angus 1970), a scale measuring extrapyramidal symptoms such as tremor and cog-wheeling; and (3) the Global Assessment Scale (GAS) (Spitzer et al. 1976), a 100-point scale, with defined anchors for every 10 points, which combines the assessment of psychopathological symptoms and social adjustment.

Assessments of social/vocational functioning were made based upon Social Adjustment Scale interviews with the patient, as well as with a close family member or significant other. These ratings were obtained at baseline, midpoint, and termination. The rater who interviewed the subject and the family member was a trained research assistant.

Criteria for Remission and Relapse

Crucial to this study are the criteria for remission and relapse because the subject must have been in remission for entry and must have met criteria for relapse as a major outcome measure. We defined remission (or partial remission) as a score of 35 or higher on the GAS and, on the BPRS, a score of no more than 4 on the items for conceptual disorganization and hallucinatory behavior, no more than 5 on the item for suspiciousness, and no more than 3 on the item for unusual thought content. The BPRS items have 7 scale points and do not have definitions for these points for each item. To increase reliability on these items used in our definition of remission, we added the anchor definition adapted from the Schedule for Affective Disorders and Schizophrenia (Endicott and Spitzer 1978).

The criteria for relapse used the same items from the BPRS as used to define remission. For those patients entering with scores two or more points below the maximum allowable, an increase in any item to the maximum allowable for entry into the study was considered to indicate relapse. For subjects who entered the study with baseline ratings at or one point below the threshold, relapse was defined as an increase of two or more rating points on any of the items.

Subjects were removed from the study if they had two psychotic relapses, had an episode of depression or mania, made a suicide attempt, missed two consecutive appointments, developed tardive dyskinesia, or had severe extrapyramidal side effects not relieved by an antiparkinsonian drug.

These criteria for remission and relapse focus completely on psychotic symptoms. We recognize that schizophrenia includes symptoms that are not psychotic. We use the psychotic symptoms because it is these which are known to respond to medication and which reasonably might be expected to show a difference between dosages of drug. Another reason to use psychotic symptoms for these criteria is to be most certain. The nonpsychotic symptoms of schizophrenia are not specific.

It is not known which clearly presage a resurgence of psychotic symptoms. For example, anxiety, social withdrawal, and insomnia are common symptoms before and during a psychotic episode. If it was certain that they predictably were prodromal symptoms, it would be a useful strategy to test whether altering drug treatment at the appearance of these symptoms would prevent the emergence of psychotic symptoms. We chose not to alter treatment or define relapse or remission by these possible prodromal symptoms to be more sure of the diagnosis.

RESULTS

Description of Subjects

The combined number of subjects among the three centers was 126. Table 1 presents information about their demographic features and the characteristics of their psychiatric histories. The majority of the subjects from NYS Psychiatric Institute were older, black or Hispanic, and ill for a longer period of time than subjects from the other two samples. On most characteristics measured at baseline, randomization successfully accomplished its task of assigning comparable subjects to the two treatment groups. There were two exceptions to a statistically significant extent. At Mount Sinai, low-dose subjects were older than standard-dose subjects, and at Hillside, standard-dose subjects were in remission for a longer period.

Relapse Rates

Among the 62 patients given low doses, 26 relapsed 31 times, 7 of whom required hospitalization. Of the 64 given standard doses, only 3 patients relapsed a total of 4 times, and none required hospitalization.

A life table graph (Figure 1) shows that 56 percent of those receiving low doses relapsed compared to 7 percent of those given standard doses. This difference is statistically significant ($p < .001$).

Most of the relapsers in both treatment groups responded quickly to adjunctive neuroleptic medication and did not require hospitalization. The relapses did not seriously disrupt the patients' social and vocational functioning. Fewer than 10 percent received benzodiazepines. Data on the use of antiparkinsonian agents are not yet available.

Predictors of Relapse

Neither baseline psychopathology, which varied little, nor length of time from hospital discharge to entry into the study correlated with outcome to a statistically significant extent.

Dosage Received

Because there was a substantially larger relapse rate among subjects on low doses, it might have been possible for these subjects

Table 1 Demographic Characteristics and Psychiatric History

	Mean	±	SD
Age (years)	28.9	±	7.1
Education [a]	3.6	±	1.1
Age at first hospitalization (years)	22.8	±	5.2
Number of hospitalizations	3.2	±	1.9
Number of weeks from hospital discharge to study entry	63.9	±	78.5
	N		(%)
Sex			
Male	79		(63)
Female	47		(37)
Race			
White	78		(61)
Black	26		(21)
Hispanic	21		(17)
Other	1		(1)
Marital Status			
Never married	98		(78)
Married	13		(10)
Divorced/widowed	15		(12)

[a] By Hollingshead Redlich Index.

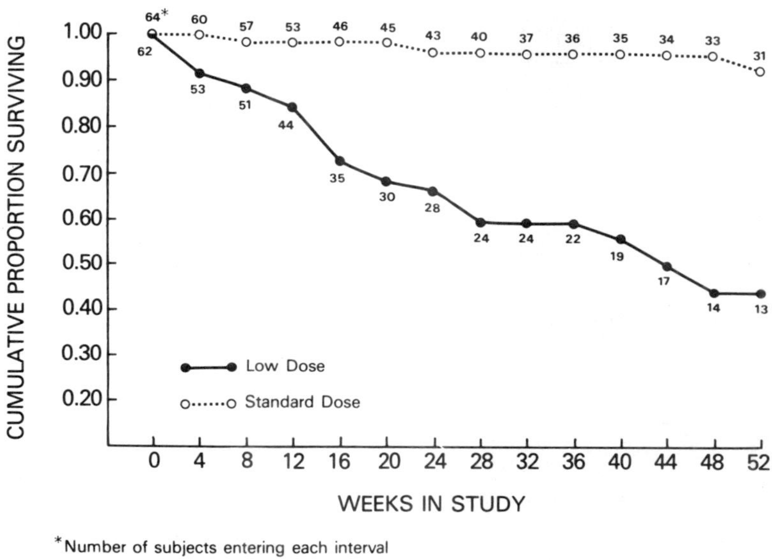

Figure 1 Survival curves over 52-week period for patients receiving low-dose or standard-dose fluphenazine decanoate therapy.

to receive adjunctive medication to the extent of reducing the difference in dosage between these two groups. The low-dose subjects who would receive the highest dose are those who relapsed but completed the entire year. The standard-dose subjects who would have received the lowest dose are those who completed a full year without relapsing. Ten of the former and 20 of the latter from the Hillside sample were compared. This low-dose group had substantially less ($p < .05$) cumulative FD than the standard-dose subjects: 400 vs 687.5 mg. Thus, there was not an overlap in dosage between the low-dose and the standard-dose subjects.

Dyskinetic Symptoms

Subjects were rated every 12 weeks with a modified version of the Simpson Dyskinesia Scale. As shown in Table 2, based only on the Hillside sample, and on all subjects who completed at least 24 weeks in the study, subjects given low doses had fewer dyskinetic symptoms than subjects given standard doses ($p = .026$). Six

Table 2 Simpson Dyskinesia Scale: Total Score at Baseline and Endpoint for Hillside Sample

	Low Dose (N = 25)		Standard Dose (N = 26)		
	Mean	SD	Mean	SD	*p*
Baseline	0.64	1.07	0.31	0.88	NS
Endpoints [a]	0.52	1.00	1.04	2.42	0.26[b]

Note. All patients who completed at least 24 weeks in the study were included.
[a] Defined as 52 weeks; otherwise, most recent rating between 24 and 52 weeks was used.
[b] By analysis of covariance, endpoint score by treatment with baseline score, as covariate *p* value is one-tailed.

subjects were judged clinically to have tardive dyskinesia: four in the standard-dose group and two in the low-dose group.

Social Adjustment

Thus far, only preliminary analyses of the social adjustment measures have been conducted (Kreisman et al. 1984; Rifkin et al. 1983).

Briefly, analyses of the patients' reports at endpoint (52 weeks, or 39 or more weeks for patients who terminated earlier) suggested that on most variables, there were no significant differences between the low-dose and standard-dose treatments. Interestingly, for almost all variables, the direction of the results indicated that low-dose patients reported themselves as doing better than the standard-dose patients. These differences reached significance on two measures of role functioning.

The results for the SAS-Family showed similar trends, with low-dose patients nonsignificantly better than standard-dose patients on most variables at endpoint. Family informants reported significantly more satisfaction with certain aspects of low-dose patients' functioning.

Comparisons were also made on endpoint SAS variables between low-dose and standard-dose patients who remained stable (did not relapse) throughout the study period, and between each of these groups and patients who relapsed. Stable low-dose patients reported better social adjustment than stable standard-dose patients at endpoint, significantly so in areas of role function and on some social items. Family reports indicated more satisfaction with stable low-dose patients than with stable standard-dose patients. In addition, these analyses suggest that, while there are significant differences on SAS-Family measures between stable low-dose patients and patients who relapsed, stable standard-dose patients are not significantly different at endpoint from patients who relapsed at some time during the study.

DISCUSSION

With subjects who are in or close to remission for the psychotic symptoms of schizophrenia, two widely varying doses of FD given for up to 12 months resulted in some important differences. The relapse rate is substantially greater among low-dose subjects. It is clear that such a low dose (1.25 to 5.0 mg every 2 weeks) is not at all comparable to standard doses in preventing relapse.

As if to balance this result, however, the low-dose group appears to function somewhat better socially. This is clearest for the low-dose patients who remained stable throughout the study period. In addition, there were fewer dyskinetic symptoms among subjects receiving low doses, suggesting that there would have been less tardive dyskinesia with low doses had we observed our subjects for a longer time or studied more of them.

We think these results have several implications. On the practical side, they show that the price of potentially improving social functioning and/or reducing the risk of tardive dyskinesia with a low dose is to increase the risk of relapse. The treating psychiatrist, patient, and family must assess the risk-benefit ratio of using this strategy. Most relapses were not devastatingly disruptive; most did not require hospitalization. The subjects were nonpsychotic again, or at their baseline, within several weeks of receiving adjunctive neuroleptic medication. Yet, for some patients the increased risk may be considered unacceptable.

Ideally the goal should be to identify patients who are likely to do well on low doses. We are exploring drug metabolism factors, as well as social and psychological factors, that may prove to have predictive value. In addition, studies using an intermediate dosage, which may produce better results, are currently underway.

The indication that social adjustment is affected by dosage of a neuroleptic suggests that poor social adjustment should join the long list of adverse reactions to neuroleptics. What might be the mechanism of this effect? We assume that the major burden should fall on the extrapyramidal side effect of akinesia. It suggests anew that akinesia should not be thought of as limited to a few neurological signs, such as diminished arm swing while walking, slow arm dropping, and slow gait, but should include complex behavior as well, such as social behavior. Since antiparkinsonian drugs were prescribed in this study, when the treating psychiatrist considered that extrapyramidal side effects might be present (data concerning their use have not yet been analysed), it suggests that such drugs cannot be counted on to control akinesia, although they help and should be tried.

References

Endicott J, Spitzer R: A diagnostic interview: the schedule for affective disorders and schizophrenia. Arch Gen Psychiatry 25:837–844, 1978

Guy W (ed): ECDEU Assessment Manual. DHEW Publication ADM 76–338. Washington, DC, US Government Printing Office, 1976

Kreisman D, Blumenthal R, Kane JM, et al: Patient and family response to standard and low doses of medication in outpatient schizophrenics. Unpublished poster presented at meeting of the American Psychopathological Association, held in New York in 1984

Overall J, Gorham D: Brief psychiatric rating scale. Psychol Rep 10:799–812, 1962

Rifkin A, Quitkin F, Rabiner CJ, et al: Fluphenazine decanoate, fluphenazine hydrochloride given orally, and placebo in remitted schizophrenics. Arch Gen Psychiatry 34:43–47, 1977

Rifkin A, Kane J, Woerner, et al: Low-dose treatments: side effects and social adjustment. Unpublished paper presented at meeting of the American Psychiatric Association, held in New York in 1983

Simpson GM, Angus JSW: A rating scale for extrapyramidal side effects. Acta Psychiatr Scand (Suppl) 212:11–19, 1970

Simpson GM, Lee JH, Zoubak B, et al.: Rating scale for tardive dyskinesia. Psychopharmacology 64:171–179, 1979

Spitzer RL, Gibbon M, Endicott J: Global Assessment Scale, in ECDEU Assessment Manual. DHEW Publication ADM 76-338. Edited by Guy W. Washington, DC, US Government Printing Office, 1976, p 583–585

Spitzer RL, Endicott J, Robins E: Research Diagnostic Criteria (RDC) for a Selected Group of Functional Disorders, 3rd ed. New York, New York State Psychiatric Institute, 1977

3

Maintenance Therapy in Schizophrenia: New Findings

Stephen R. Marder, M.D.
Theodore Van Putten, M.D.
Jim Mintz, Ph.D.
Malca Lebell, Ph.D.
Joanne McKenzie, R.N.
Gary Faltico, Ph.D.

3

Maintenance Therapy in Schizophrenia: New Findings

The maintenance phase of treatment begins after a schizophrenic patient has recovered from a psychotic episode. At this point, the clinician faces new problems. During the acute psychotic phase, the most dramatic symptoms of schizophrenia, such as hallucinations, delusions, and thought disorder, usually dominate the clinical picture. During the maintenance phase, these symptoms are of lesser significance and a new set of problems emerge: namely, the negative schizophrenic impairments, such as affective flattening, avolition, asociality, and attentional impairments. Thus the goals of maintenance therapy are twofold: first, to prevent the recurrence of exacerbation of positive symptoms and, second, to minimize negative impairments.

Effectiveness of Drug Maintenance

Experience with maintenance neuroleptic drugs over the years has indicated that drugs have powerful effects insofar as preventing or delaying relapse. Davis (1975) reviewed 24 double-blind studies of

---

Supported by the Veterans Administration Medical Research Service and the Mental Health Clinical Research Center for the Study of Schizophrenia (UCLA).

maintenance therapy and found that in all studies many more patients relapsed on placebo than on drug. When the results of the studies were pooled, 698 (65 percent) of the 1,068 patients on placebo relapsed in contrast to only 639 (30 percent) of the 2,127 patients on drug. This powerful drug effect provides the scientific basis for continuing most schizophrenic patients on long-term neuroleptic maintenance even after they appear to have recovered from a psychotic episode.

Among schizophrenic patients, merely remaining unrelapsed is very different from doing well. Discharged schizophrenic patients often adjust poorly in the community. One study (Schooler et al. 1967) found that only 11 percent of schizophrenic patients discharged on drug functioned at the level of the average person in the community. These patients are commonly unemployed or supported by some type of public assistance. Even when patients are able to work, they are often confined to the lowest paying, most menial jobs as a result of their illness.

Thus drugs in remitted patients prevent relapse, but they often fail to have major effects on the negative impairments that have such an importance influence on the adjustment of schizophrenic patients.

ADVERSE EFFECTS OF MAINTENANCE NEUROLEPTICS

Chronic administration of neuroleptics appears to be more toxic than was initially believed. Tardive dyskinesias are probably the most serious problems associated with neuroleptic therapy in the sense that the only treatment—early discontinuation of antipsychotic drugs—is usually not feasible. These dyskinesias usually consist of mouth and tongue movements, such as lip smacking and puckering, as well as facial grimacing and irregular movements of the limbs, trunk, and fingers. Although seriously disabling dyskinesias are uncommon, a small percentage may affect walking, breathing, eating, and talking. At least 10 to 20 percent of patients treated with neuroleptics for more than a year develop tardive dyskinesias (Task Force Report 1980). Although most of the resulting abnormal movements are mild, the large number of individuals affected has made this disorder an important public health problem.

There are other pressures on psychiatrists to reduce the amount of neuroleptic drug that patients receive. Clinicians have recently begun to appreciate that extrapyramidally based side effects can make schizophrenic patients feel miserable. It is important to emphasize that schizophrenic patients in maintenance therapy form a group of individuals who endure considerable suffering. Even when patients have been relieved of the most dramatic schizophrenic symptoms—as they often are during the maintenance phase of treatment—they continue to complain of symptoms usually thought to characterize anxious and depressed patients. Depression is a particularly serious problem and may occur either during relapse or when psychotic symptoms are well controlled. More than one-half of schizophrenic patients experience clinically significant depressions during the course of maintenance therapy. The risk of a new episode of depression is three times as great as the risk of a relapse of psychosis. Moreover, the duration of morbidity from depression is longer than that from schizophrenic symptoms (Johnson 1981). The problem of anxiety in maintenance patients is likely to be of a similar magnitude.

Some of this misery may be worsened by drugs. Two of the most common extrapyramidal side effects, akathesia and akinesia, have the potential for causing dysphorias by themselves. Akathesia, the most common extrapyramidal side effect, is defined as a subjective feeling of restlessness. In a recent study (Van Putten et al. in press), 40 percent of patients receiving haloperidol experienced akathesia. Most were evaluated as being moderate to very severe. The akathesia experienced by patients correlated with their self-rated amount of anxiety. This is consistent with previous reports by Van Putten (1974) in which he has described the anguish of patients who complain of a continuing feeling of restlessness and their inability to find any comfort or rest.

Akinesia has been defined by Rifkin et al. (1977) as a behavioral state characterized by decreased expressive gestures, diminished speech, and a disinterest in one's usual activities. Since these symptoms bear a striking resemblance to the flattened affect and motivation that characterize the negative impairments of schizophrenia, it is easy to understand why they frequently go unrecognized. Van Putten and May (1978) have described a group of schizophrenic patients who develop akinesia. Although these patients became less psychotic, they also experienced a significant increase in depression ratings. Van Putten and May have described a syndrome which they call akinetic depression and have implied that a depressed mood could conceivably be a side effect associated with neuroleptic treatment. It should be mentioned that some of the patients they described complained of the hopelessness and despondency so characteristic of clinical depression. These patients often felt less depressed when they were adequately treated with antiparkinson medications.

Drug-induced akinesia may be a particular concern when patients are treated with fluphenazine decanoate (FD). This is the only neuroleptic available in the United States that can be administered in a long-acting depot form. It is therefore one of the most commonly prescribed drugs for patients in maintenance therapy. In one study, Rifkin et al. (1977a) found that 35 percent of those patients assigned to FD developed disabling akinesia. Hogarty et al. (1979) found that patients who relapsed on FD experienced more anxiety and depression than did patients who relapsed on oral fluphenazine.

NEW STRATEGIES FOR MAINTENANCE THERAPY

All of these problems with maintenance therapy have led researchers to consider methods for decreasing the total amount of neuroleptic drug that patients receive. At the present time, two particular strategies are under active investigation. The first proposes treating patients intermittently with neuroleptics. The other, the low dose strategy, proposes treating patients with much lower neuroleptic doses than most psychiatrists are used to prescribing.

Intermittent Therapy

Carpenter et al. (1982) and Herz et al. (1982) have proposed gradually decreasing the amount of drug that stable patients receive until medications are completely discontinued. Patients are then followed very closely until there are signs that the individual is beginning to relapse. At this time, drugs are reinstituted. To make this strategy work, patients and their families are trained to detect prodromal signs of impending psychotic breakdown. Their preliminary findings indicate that this is a promising method.

Low Dose Treatment

Goldstein et al. (1978) were among the first to explore the effectiveness of low doses of neuroleptic. In a study that combined family and drug treatment, they assigned outpatients to either 6.25 or 25 mg of fluphenazine enanthate administered intramuscularly every 2 weeks. (Most patients receiving long acting fluphenazine are administered 25 mg or more every 2 weeks.) The higher dose provided more protection against relapse during the 6-week trial period. Good premorbid patients, however, were more anxious on the higher dose, suggesting that some patients paid a price for this protection. Because relapse rates were low in good premorbids on both doses, the findings suggest that the lower dose may constitute a reasonable treatment regimen for at least some patients.

In a more recent study, Kane et al. (1983) treated stabilized outpatients with dosages of FD between 1.25 and 5 mg every 2 weeks. Most patients on this regimen remained remitted for 6 months. A subgroup of the remitted patients were later randomized double-blind to either the same low dose or a placebo. Relapse rates on the lower dose were significantly lower than on placebo. In a subsequent study, patients were randomized in a double-blind comparison of two dose ranges of FD (1.25 to 5 mg versus 12.5 to 50 mg every 2 weeks). Relapse rates were significantly higher in the low dose group (56 percent) than in the standard dose group (7 percent). As in the Goldstein et al. (1978) study, however, there were disadvantages associated with the higher dose. Low dose patients had a better outcome in terms of certain measures of social adjustment as well as lower dyskinesia ratings.

With these prior studies in mind, we designed a study to

evaluate both the costs and benefits of a low and conventional dose of FD. Our study differed from that of Kane et al. (1983) in that two fixed doses of FD were selected: 5 mg as the low dose and 25 mg as the conventional dose. Thus our low dose of 5 mg was substantially more than their low dose range of 1.25 to 5 mg. We were interested in answering two questions: Will relapse rates be substantially increased by maintaining patients on only 5 mg of FD, and will there be advantages associated with the lower dose, such as fewer side effects or enhanced feelings of well being?

STUDY DESCRIPTION

The subjects were outpatients referred to a specialized research clinic at a large urban Veterans Administration Medical Center. All met DSM-III criteria for a diagnosis of schizophrenic disorder, and their symptomatic profiles were elicited from the Present State Examination. Subjects were stabilized for 2 or more months on FD. Individuals who required more than 25 mg every 2 weeks were dropped. Other exclusion criteria included organic brain disease and severe alcoholism or other substance abuse.

After the stabilization period, all neuroleptics were stopped for 4 weeks. This actually entailed missing one biweekly injection. Patients were then randomized to a double-blind trial of either 5 or 25 mg every 2 weeks. Each patient received 1 cc of a solution that contained either 5 or 25 mg of FD. Antiparkinsonian drugs—usually 2 to 4 mg of benztropine twice daily—were prescribed whenever extrapyramidal symptoms emerged or whenever they had been a serious problem in the past.

Patients were maintained on their assigned dose for as long as their condition was stable. We characterized two levels of unfavorable outcome, which compelled a dosage adjustment. The less severe was designated a psychotic exacerbation and occurred when patients demonstrated a worsening of 3 or more on Brief Psychiatric Rating Scale (BPRS) cluster scores for thought disturbance or paranoia. The protocol would then allow the treating psychiatrist to increase the drug dose up to 2 cc. In other words, the low dose patients who had psychotic exacerbations on 5 mg could have

Table 1 Demographic Characteristics

	5 mg FD (N = 28)			25 mg FD (N = 22)		
	Mean	±	SD	Mean	±	SD
Age (years)	35.4	±	9.0	37.2	±	7.7
Education (years)	12.9	±	1.6	12.5	±	2.0
Illness Duration (months)	146	±	95	168	±	90
Age of Onset (years)	23.5	±	4.6	23.4	±	4.1
	N	%		N	%	
Race						
White	8	(28.6)		9	(40.9)	
Black	17	(60.7)		11	(50.0)	
Hispanic	1	(3.6)		2	(9.1)	
Other	2	(7.2)		0	(0.0)	
Marital Status						
Single	15	(53.6)		13	(59.1)	
Married	6	(21.4)		2	(9.1)	
Divorced	3	(10.7)		5	(22.7)	
Separated	4	(14.3)		2	(9.1)	

their dose of FD increased to 10 mg, whereas those on 25 mg could receive as much as 50 mg.

Table 1 describes the background characteristics of the 50 patients included in this report. Notably, a majority of the patients were both Black and single. Nearly all patients were unemployed and had severely impaired social relations. Patients in this study were chronic schizophrenic patients who had been ill for an average of more than 10 years.

Survival Rates

Figure 1 is a survival curve that displays the proportion of patients in each group who remained unexacerbated on 5 or 25 mg of FD during the first year of treatment. Patients who had an increase in symptoms that was controlled by an increase in dose to as much as 10 mg in the low dose group and 50 mg in the conventional dose group were nevertheless considered to have had an exacerbation. Therefore, this figure underestimates survival

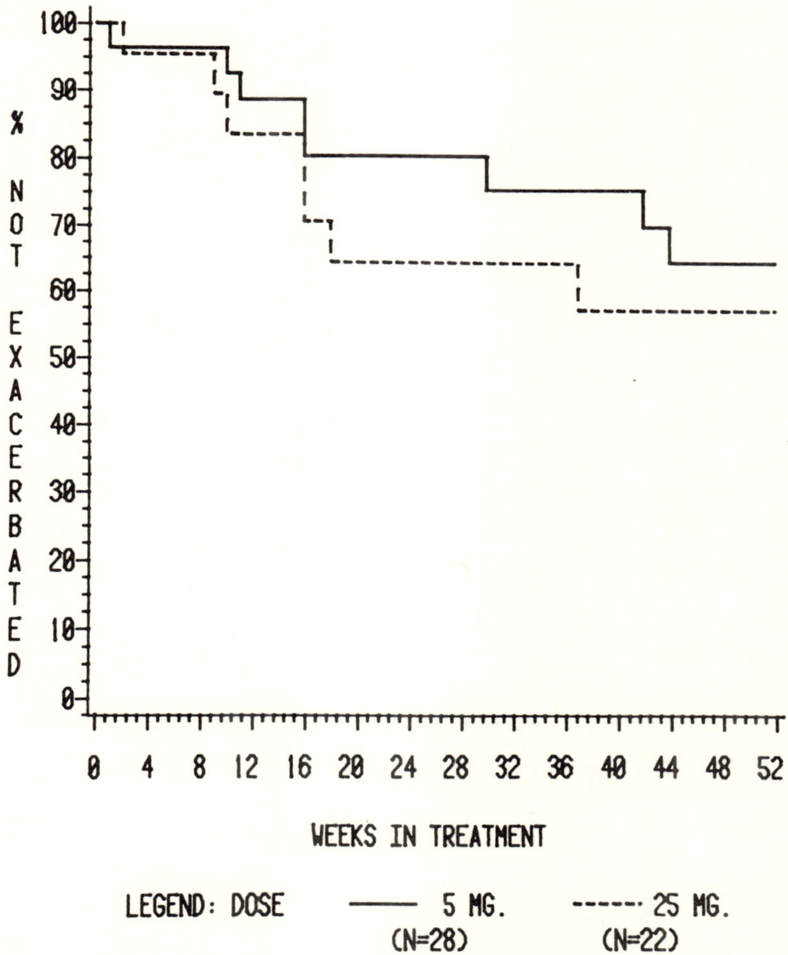

Figure 1 Survival analysis of psychotic exacerbations for patients receiving 5 or 25 mg of fluphenazine decanoate every 14 days. Survival was computed using BMDP statistical software (Dixon 1981).

because only the protective power of the original assigned dose is evaluated. The difference in survival rates on the two doses was not statistically significant. Actual 1-year survivals were 64.5 percent on 5 mg and 57.1 percent on 25 mg.

Using the same analysis, Figure 2 represents the patients surviv-

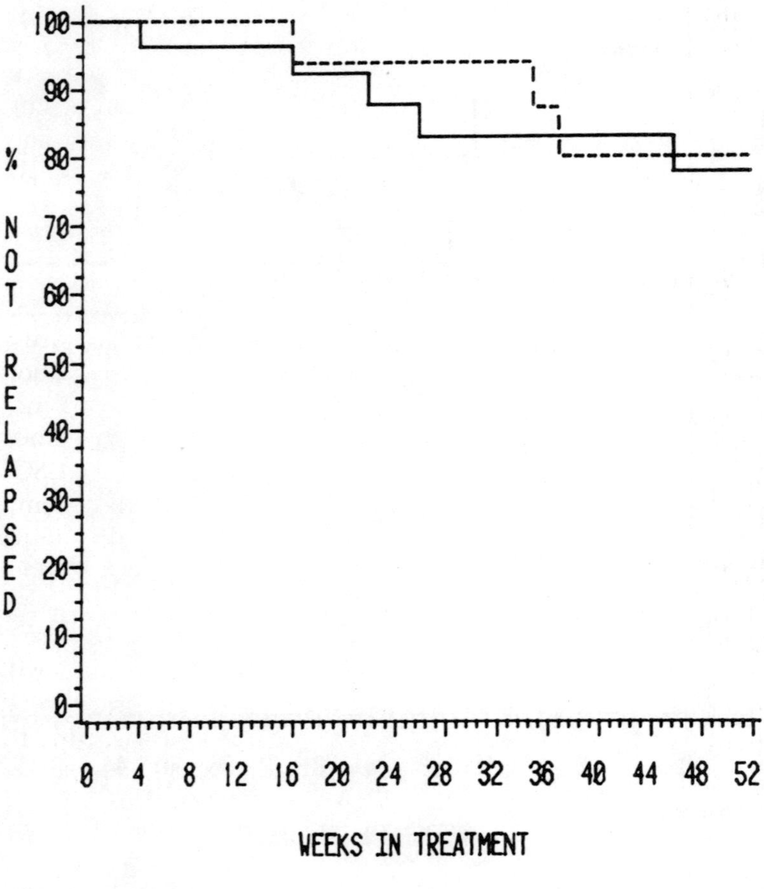

Figure 2 Survival analysis of relapses for patients receiving 5 or 25 mg of fluphenazine decanoate every 14 days. Survival was computed using BMDP statistical software (Dixon 1981).

ing unrelapsed. Patients were considered survivors if they could be managed within the dose ranges of 5 to 10 mg or 25 to 50 mg. The actual 1-year survival rates were 77.6 percent on the lower dose range and 79.8 percent on the higher dose range. Again, the difference was not statistically significant.

If we can assume survival rates on placebo would be about 35 percent, as they have been in nearly every placebo study of maintenance therapy, then both doses appear to be active in preventing relapse. Looking at group data, however, can obscure what happens in individual cases. We did find at least four patients randomized to the 5 mg dose who could not be restabilized until they were returned to more conventional doses.

Symptoms and Self-Rated Distress

We also examined the clinical state of patients who survived at each time point without having suffered a relapse or exacerbation. There were no differences in clinical psychopathology as measured by the BPRS in patients surviving on 5 and 25 mg. There were differences, however, in their SCL-90 factor scores. (The SCL-90 is a self-rated inventory of subjective feeling states.) At 1 month, all of the factors were elevated in the patients assigned to 25 mg (Table 2). Differences were significant on the obsessive-compulsive, interpersonal sensitivity, depression, and phobic anxiety scales. At 3 months (Table 3), with a smaller sample because of drop-out and relapses, the data have the same appearance, with higher factor scores for obsessive-compulsive, interpersonal sensitivity, and phobic anxiety. It appears that patients assigned to the

Table 2 SCL-90 Factor Scores at 1 Month

	5 mg FD (N = 26)			25 mg FD (N = 21)		
	Mean	±	SD	Mean	±	SD
Somatization	.53	±	.83	.63	±	.57
Obsessive-Compulsive	.70	±	.89	1.12	±	.72*
Interpersonal Sensitivity	.56	±	.74	1.00	±	.70**
Depression	.70	±	.69	1.02	±	.78*
Anxiety	.61	±	.68	.89	±	.87
Anger-Hostility	.26	±	.40	.49	±	.60
Phobic Anxiety	.40	±	.73	.71	±	.67*
Paranoid Ideation	.77	±	.92	.93	±	.74
Psychoticism	.73	±	.74	.96	±	.78

Note. Covariate adjusted means. Baseline value for each item was used as covariate.
$^{*}p < .05$.
$^{**}p < .01$.

Table 3 SCL-90 Factor Scores at 3 Months

	5 mg FD (N = 23)			25 mg FD (N = 12)		
	Mean	±	SD	Mean	±	SD
Somatization	.51	±	.61	.54	±	.43
Obsessive-Compulsive	.60	±	.89	1.02	±	.79
Interpersonal Sensitivity	.50	±	.86	.94	±	.64*
Depression	.61	±	.68	1.00	±	.73
Anxiety	.50	±	.59	.80	±	.65
Anger-Hostility	.25	±	.40	.38	±	.36
Phobic Anxiety	.36	±	.72	.87	±	.67*
Paranoid Ideation	.83	±	.86	.79	±	.71
Psychoticism	.76	±	.83	.91	±	.75

Note. Covariate adjusted means. Baseline value for each item was used as covariate.
$^*p < .05$.

Table 4 Side Effect Factors at 1 Month

	5 mg FD (N = 26)			25 mg FD (N = 20)		
	Mean	±	SD	Mean	±	SD
Akinesia	.78	±	1.22	.98	±	1.51
Retardation	1.59	±	2.02	1.64	±	1.41
Tardive Dyskinesia	.44	±	.79	.64	±	.86
Akathesia	1.58	±	1.81	1.87	±	1.73

Note. Covariate adjusted means. Baseline value for each item was used as covariate.

Table 5 Side Effect Factors at 3 Months

	5 mg FD (N = 23)			25 mg FD (N = 12)		
	Mean	±	SD	Mean	±	SD
Akinesia	.83	±	1.28	1.27	±	1.28
Retardation	1.12	±	1.45	2.24	±	1.73*
Tardive Dyskinesia	.56	±	.85	.69	±	.56
Akathesia	.79	±	1.28	1.90	±	1.48*

Note. Covariate adjusted means. Baseline value for each item was used as covariate.
$^*p < .05$.

higher dose were paying a price for the higher dose in that they reported greater subjective distress.

Could this discomfort be related to side effects? The side effect factors in Tables 4 and 5 are derived from a factor analysis of our subjective and objective side effect scales. At 1 month (Table 4), there were no differences between the two groups, although you will note slightly higher scores for the higher dose. At 3 months (Table 5), the trend becomes clearer, with significant differences appearing for akathesia and retardation. Table 6 displays correlations at 3 months between the retardation and akathesia side effect factors and the SCL-90 factors. These correlations suggest that side effects can increase a patient's subjective experience of anxiety and depression.

It is important to know whether these statistically significant differences in personal distress are really of clinical importance. We believe that they are for a number of reasons. In the first place, schizophrenic patients in maintenance treatment begin at a high level of personal distress. Whether this is a primary manifestation of the illness or secondary to poverty and humiliation, these individuals, on medication or not, commonly feel dysphoric. It is sobering to think that our treatments can add to this misery. In addition, recent findings regarding the treatment of chronic

Table 6 Correlations Between Side Effects and SCL-90 Factors, Ratings at 3 Months

	Retardation	Akathesia
Somatization	.298	.246
Obsessive-Compulsive	.380*	.288
Interpersonal Sensitivity	.339*	.327
Depression	.601****	.409*
Anxiety	.391*	.431**
Anger-Hostility	.267	.303
Phobic Anxiety	.437**	.555***
Paranoid Ideation	.195	.265
Psychoticism	.229	.157

*$p < .05$.
**$p < .01$.
***$p < .001$.
****$p < .0001$.

schizophrenia indicate that patients will benefit the most from programs that include the protective influence of drugs as well as psychosocial treatments, such as family therapy, individual psychotherapy, and social skills training. These psychological treatments are likely to affect the negative schizophrenic impairments that are relatively refractory to the influence of medications. It is conceivable that an inappropriate pharmacotherapy that causes patients to feel anxious, depressed, and despondent could have a ripple effect that makes other modes of treatment more difficult.

We also found another clinical manifestation of a high distress level, that is, a higher dropout rate. Seven patients, five of whom had been assigned to the higher dose, dropped out during the first year. Patients who dropped out on the higher dose rated themselves particularly high on the SCL-90.

We interpret our findings as indicating that patients who are in treatment with conventional doses of maintenance neuroleptic have a good chance of doing just as well on much lower doses. There is also a reasonable chance that patients will do better with less drug. They may feel better and, as a result, may be more likely to stay in treatment.

Prodromal Signs of Relapse

As mentioned previously, one method proposed for preventing relapse requires detecting early signs that a patient is relapsing. Docherty et al. (1978) proposed that schizophrenic relapse is a process with stages that unfold in a recognizable pattern. More recently, Herz and Melville (1980) reported that schizophrenic patients and their families are usually aware of a prodromal period that precedes relapse.

To confirm these reports, we used data from the previously described study of 5 and 25 mg of FD to investigate the events that preceded relapse. We analyzed the SCL-90 and BPRS ratings of 41 patients, 14 of whom relapsed. We compared the 14 rating occasions that preceded these relapses with 61 occasions that did not precede relapse in these same patients and with 180 rating

Table 7 Change in BPRS Factor Scores Just Prior to Relapse Compared with Average Change

	Nonrelapsers (N = 27; 180 observations)			Relapsers (N = 14; 61 observations [a]			Relapsers (N = 14; 14 observations) [b]		
Factor	Mean	±	SD	Mean	±	SD	Mean	±	SD
Thought Disorder	−0.15	±	2.12	−0.25	±	1.85	1.79	±	1.39*
Depression	−0.16	±	2.34	−0.36	±	2.93	2.29*	±	2.70
Paranoid	−0.09	±	1.17	−0.07	±	1.46	1.50	±	1.91**
Retardation	0.02	±	1.54	−0.28	±	2.1	−0.36	±	2.21

Note Change in successive observations. Positive values indicate worsening.
[a] Observations not preceding relapse.
[b] Observations just preceding relapse.
$^{*}p < .01$.
$^{**}p < .001$.

Table 8 Change in SCL-90 Factor Scores Just Prior to Relapse Compared with Average Change

	Nonrelapsers (N = 27; 180 observations)			Relapsers (N = 14; 61 observations [a]			Relapsers (N = 14; 14 observations) [b]		
Factor	Mean	±	SD	Mean	±	SD	Mean	±	SD
Somatizaton	− .01	±	.42	−.00	±	3.2	.05	±	.35
Obsessive-Compulsive	− .02	±	.54	−0.7	±	.48	.33	±	.72
Interpersonal-Sensitivity	− .03	±	.46	−.02	±	.48	.31	±	.62*
Depression	− .04	±	.48	−.10	±	.48	.36	±	.65*
Anxiety	− .03	±	.47	−.08	±	.33	.36	±	.42**
Anger-Hostility	− .02	±	.46	−.02	±	.40	.26	±	.44
Phobic-Anxiety	− .02	±	.41	−.04	±	.42	.24	±	.56
Paranoid Ideation	− .08	±	.59	−.05	±	.56	.50	±	.73**
Psychoticism	− .05	±	.46	−.06	±	.40	.45	±	.53***

Note Average change in successive observations. Positive values represent worsening.
[a] Observations not preceding relapse.
[b] Observations just preceding relapse.
$^{*}p < .05$.
$^{**}p < .01$.
$^{***}p < .001$.

occasions for patients who never relapsed. Ratings were first converted to successive differences by subtracting from each the rating obtained at the previous evaluation. To control for the point in time at which each observation was made, difference scores were converted to standard scores (mean, 0; SD, 1) based on the change scores for all patients at that rating occasion. Table 7 shows average change (not standardized) for each set of occasions. For the occasions that did not precede relapse, there was a negligible change. Prior to relapse, there was a significant change in BPRS cluster scores for depression, thought disturbance, and paranoia. The prerelapse occasion occurred from 1 to 12 weeks prior to relapse, with the mean being about 4 weeks. These mean changes were very small, equaling about two points on a 21-point range. We believe that these small changes would have gone unrecognized by most clinicians in most cases. SCL-90 factor scores for interpersonal sensitivity, depression, anxiety, paranoid ideation, and psychoticism were also elevated prior to relapse (Table 8).

We then used a stepwise discriminant function analysis to determine which factors best discriminated between the 241 occasions in which relapse did not occur and the 14 that preceded relapse. The most discriminating items included the paranoid and depression factors from the BPRS and the psychoticism factor from the SCL-90. Figure 3 represents the distribution of change scores on these three items. The weights yielded by the discriminant analysis were rounded off for ease in clinical use. None of the 14 relapses occurred after patients improved on the two BPRS clusters. Nearly all of the relapses occurred after a patient had worsened on both the BPRS and SCL-90 items. This demonstrates that such a formula, if used in a clinic, could probably predict most relapses, although there would be a considerable number of cases in which relapse would have been falsely predicted, i.e., false positives.

These findings indicate that clinicians should be concerned about even minor worsenings in the condition of schizophrenic patients who are in maintenance therapy, particularly when these involve thought disturbance, depression, paranoia, and personal distress. When such prodromal signs appear, it would seem appropriate for clinicians to consider an intervention that might

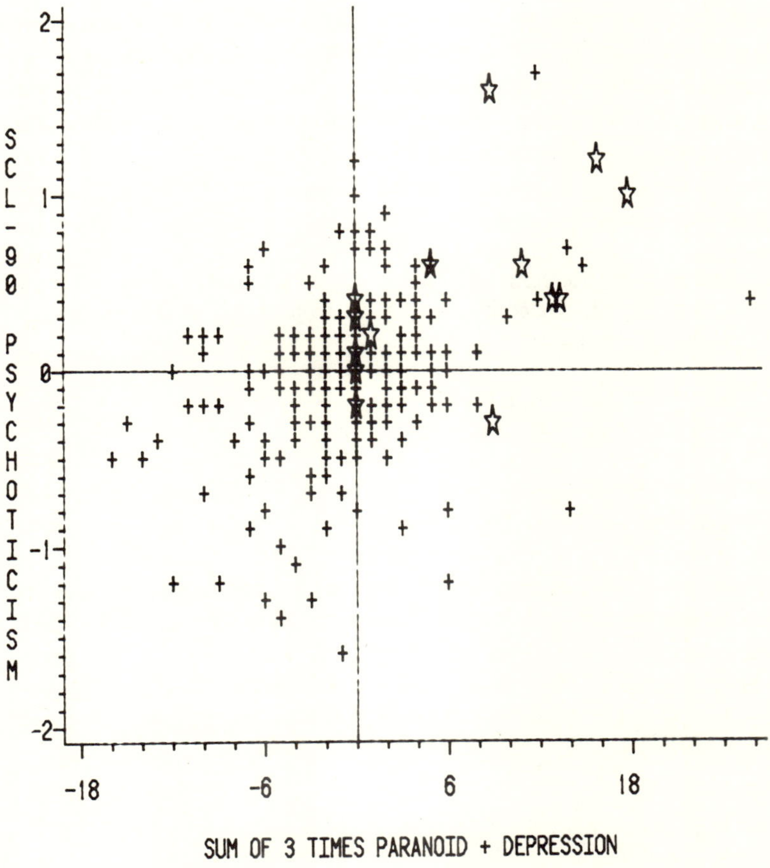

Figure 3 Distribution of change scores for 255 rating occasions. Assessments that did not precede relapse are indicated by a plus sign; those that did precede a relapse are indicated by a star.

prevent relapse. This might consist of dosage adjustment, a psychosocial intervention, more frequent monitoring, or a combination of these strategies.

In conclusion, our results suggest two steps that may improve the outcome of schizophrenic patients. The first involves treating the patient with a drug dose as near to the therapeutic threshold as possible. This may lead to the patient's feeling better and to improved compliance with prescribed treatment. It may also render the patient more vulnerable to relapse. Perhaps this vulnerability may be minimized by an early intervention model whereby even minor worsenings in clinical condition will trigger a response from the therapist.

References

Carpenter WT, Stephens JH, Rey AC, et al: Early intervention vs continuous pharmacotherapy of schizophrenia. Psychopharmacol Bull 18:21–23, 1982

Davis J: Overview: maintenance therapy in psychiatry, I. schizophrenia. Am J Psychiatry 132:1237–1245, 1975

Dixon WJ: BMDP Statistical Software. Berkeley, University of California Press, 1981

Docherty JP, Van Kammen DP, Siris SG, et al: Stages of onset of schizophrenic psychosis. Am J Psychiatry 135:420–426, 1978

Goldstein MS, Rodnick EM, Evans JR, et al: Drugs and family therapy in the aftercare of acute schizophrenics. Arch Gen Psychiatry 35:1169–1177, 1978

Herz MI, Melville C: Relapse in schizophrenia. Am J Psychiatry 137:801–805, 1980

Herz MI, Szymanski HV, Simon JL: Intermittent medication for stable schizophrenic outpatients: an alternative to maintenance medication. Am J Psychiatry 139:918–922, 1982

Hogarty GE, Schooler N, Ulrich RF, et al: Fluphenazine and social therapy in the aftercare of schizophrenic patients: relapse analysis of a two year controlled study of fluphenazine decanoate and fluphenazine hydrochloride. Arch Gen Psychiatry 36:1283–1294, 1979

Johnson DAW: Studies of depressive symptoms in schizophrenia. Br J Psychiatry 139:89–101, 1981

Kane JM, Rifkin A, Woerner M, et al: Low dose neuroleptic treatment of outpatient schizophrenics; I: preliminary results for relapse rates. Arch Gen Psychiatry 40:893–896, 1983

Rifkin A, Quitkin F, Klein DF: Akinesia: a poorly recognized drug-induced extrapyramidal behavioral disorder. Arch Gen Psychiatry 34:43–47, 1977a

Rifkin A, Quitkin F, Rabiner C, et al: Fluphenazine decanoate, oral fluphenazine and placebo in remitted schizophrenics; I: relapse rates after one year. Arch Gen Psychiatry 34:43–47, 1977b

Schooler N, Goldberg S, Boothe H, et al: One year after discharge: community adjustment of schizophrenic patients. Am J Psychiatry 123:989–995, 1967

Task Force Report of the American Psychiatric Association: Effects of antipsychotic drugs: tardive dyskinesia. Am J Psychiatry 137:1163–1171, 1980

Van Putten T: Why do schizophrenic patients refuse to take their drugs? Arch Gen Psychiatry 31:67–72, 1974

Van Putten T, May PRA: Akinetic depression in schizophrenia. Arch Gen Psychiatry 35:1101–1107, 1978

Van Putten T, May PRA, Marder SR: Akathesia with haloperidol and thiothixene. Arch Gen Psychiatry (in press)

4

Intermittent Medication and Schizophrenia

Marvin I. Herz, M.D.

4

Intermittent Medication and Schizophrenia

Longitudinal studies of the course of schizophrenia have shown that it is an illness characterized by exacerbations and periods of remission during which there is minor or major disability (Ciompi 1980; Huber et al. 1980; Englehardt et al. 1982). In view of the fact that many schizophrenic patients have episodic relapses, it is surprising that there has been little systematic study of early signs of relapse and the decompensation process in general. This is in contrast to most chronic physical illnesses that are marked by acute exacerbations. It is possible that psychiatry may not have addressed the question of relapse in schizophrenia because most patients in the past were housed in custodial institutions, and little attention was paid to fluctuations in the course of the illness. Because most patients now live in the community and often cause some disruption when they relapse, concern about the question of relapse and rehospitalization has increased.

My colleagues and I were concerned about the long-term deleterious effects of maintenance antipsychotic medication for schizophrenic patients. We wondered whether medication for stable outpatients could be administered intermittently, only during early signs of relapse, rather than have them maintained on medication indefinitely. Hogarty and his associates (1973) found that patients on medication who were switched to placebo did not have a steady downhill course. Instead, most patients remained in remission and their symptom patterns and severity measured cross-sectionally were similar to those of the drug patients. However, many of the placebo patients relapsed at some point during the 2 years of the study and had to be hospitalized or removed from the study and given active drug treatment. These findings and the clinical observations of other investigators seem to indicate that, for many stable schizophrenic patients, antipsychotic medication is mainly prophylactic. Thus it seemed that a strategy aimed at early intervention during the beginning of the psychotic episode might be effective in preventing full relapse from occurring.

THE PROCESS OF RELAPSE

Procedure

As a first step in exploring the feasibility of an intermittent medication approach, it seemed essential to learn more about the relapse process, especially early signs of relapse. We decided to interview schizophrenic patients and family members about the relapse process. Two groups of patients in different parts of the country were studied (Herz and Melville 1980). In Atlanta (Group A), 99 outpatients (66 women) who were being treated at two community mental health centers were interviewed. In separate interviews, 80 family informants were seen. Since these patients were stable outpatients whose psychotic episodes had occurred more than 6 months prior to the interview, we also interviewed a group of recently hospitalized patients to determine whether they would have different observations about the relapse period, given their more recent experience with a psychotic episode. Group B consisted of 46 hospitalized patients (32 women) in a county hospital in Buffalo, most of whom had been in the hospital for less than 2 weeks. Patients in Group A were diagnosed as schizophrenic according to DSM-II; DSM-III was used for Group B. All patients had been hospitalized at least two times and usually more often. The Atlanta group was primarily suburban or rural and

White. The mean age was 38 years, and the mean level of education was 10 years. Only 15 percent were employed and 33 percent were married. Approximately 73 percent had been hospitalized three or more times. The Buffalo group was largely urban; 68 percent were White, 28 percent Black, and 4 percent Puerto Rican. The mean age was 38 years and the mean level of education was 9 years. Level of employment was 26 percent and 24 percent were married. Patients were interviewed using a structured interview, the Early Signs Questionnaire, with a few open-ended questions based on items contained in the Psychiatric Status Schedule (Spitzer et al. 1968), Research Diagnostic Criteria (Spitzer et al. 1975), and on clinical experience.

Results

Approximately 70 percent of patients reported that they could tell there were changes in their thoughts, feelings, or behaviors that led them to believe they were becoming sick and might have to go to the hospital. Of great importance, 93 percent of family members indicated they noticed changes in the patient. Because relatives usually recognize early signs of decompensation, it is extremely important to involve them in therapeutic management.

The time interval between the beginning of the development of symptomatology and the need for rehospitalization is also of great clinical importance in the prevention of full relapse. If decompensation were sudden and abrupt, then therapeutic interventions could not be introduced in time to prevent the occurrence of full relapse. Only about 8 percent of patients and 11 percent of family members stated that the time period was less than 1 day. Fifteen percent of Group B patients and 8 percent of Group A patients and their families noticed a prodromal period of only 1 to 3 days. In fact, 52 percent of Group B patients, 48 percent of Group A patients, and 68 percent of families said that it took more than a week. Thus it appears that there should be ample time to intervene with crisis intervention therapies, including pharmacotherapy, after prodromal signs begin in order to abort the development of a full relapse.

A major question was whether symptoms became progressively more serious pathologically. Was there an earlier nonpsychotic prodromal period prior to development of a full-blown relapse? We asked patients to identify which symptoms either appeared for the first time or worsened during the early stage of a relapse. A remarkably similar clinical picture was reported by both groups even though the Group A patients were outpatients in relatively stable condition, and the Buffalo patients had recently experienced an acute psychotic episode and were still in the hospital. Furthermore, there were major differences between the groups demographically. The rank-order correlation of reported symptoms that appeared or worsened before hospitalization between the Buffalo and Atlanta patients was .85 ($p < .001$) (Table 1).

The symptom reported by most patients in both groups was becoming tense and nervous. In general, the symptoms most

Table 1 Symptoms That Appeared or Worsened Before Hospitalization in Schizophrenic Patients

	Buffalo Group (N = 46)	Atlanta Group	
		Patients (N = 99)	Families (N = 80)
Symptom	Rank (%)	Rank (%)	Rank (%)
Tense and nervous	1 (80.4)	1 (70.7)	1 (83.3)
Eating less	2 (71.7)	10 (49.5)	17 (52.5)
Trouble concentrating	3 (69.6)	5 (56.6)	3 (76.3)
Trouble sleeping	4 (67.4)	3 (61.6)	7 (68.8)
Enjoy things less	5 (65.2)	8 (52.5)	8 (67.5)
Restlessness	6 (63.0)	4 (58.6)	2 (78.8)
Can't remember things	6 (63.0)	14 (46.5)	10 (60.0)
Depression	8 (60.9)	2 (63.6)	3 (76.3)
Preoccupied with one or two things	9 (59.6)	12 (48.5)	9 (65.0)
Seeing friends less	9 (59.6)	7 (54.5)	18 (50.0)
Am being laughed at, talked about	9 (59.6)	9 (51.5)	14 (53.8)
Loss of interest in things	12 (56.5)	5 (56.5)	6 (73.8)
More religious thinking	13 (54.3)	10 (49.5)	19 (47.5)
Feeling bad for no reason	13 (54.3)	19 (40.4)	22 (37.5)
Feeling too excited	15 (52.2)	25 (30.3)	14 (53.8)
Hearing voices, seeing things	16 (50.0)	17 (42.4)	10 (60.0)
Feeling worthless	17 (48.8)	15 (44.5)	12 (56.3)
Talking in nonsensical way	18 (45.6)	13 (47.5)	3 (76.3)

Note. Spearman rank-order correlation for Buffalo patients and Atlanta patients = .85; and for Atlanta patients and families = .78 ($p < .001$).

frequently reported by patients and family members were of a nonpsychotic nature similar to the dysphoria that nonpsychotic individuals experience under stress, such as eating less, having trouble concentrating, having trouble sleeping, depression, and seeing friends less. The psychotic symptom most frequently reported by patients in both groups was a feeling of being laughed at or talked about. The rank-order correlation of frequency of symptoms reported by Atlanta patients and their relatives was also very high ($r = .78$, $p < .001$).

When patients were asked what were the *first* changes in thoughts, feelings, and behavior that might have led them to believe that they were becoming sick and might have to go to the hospital, there was little agreement. However, the symptoms reported are similar to those previously mentioned, i.e., tension, anxiety, nervousness, insomnia, and depression. An important issue was whether the pattern of development of an episode was similar for each episode. Fifty percent of the patients answered that there was similar development of symptom progression until full relapse. On the other hand, the other 50 percent did not notice any such pattern. Whether or not individual patients have the same sequential pattern of symptoms when they relapse is of great importance to the psychiatrist who plans treatment strategy. When treating a schizophrenic patient, the therapist should ask patients and significant others what they know about the relapse period. What are the early symptoms; is there a similar sequential pattern of development of symptoms; do relapses occur at special times during the calendar year; are they related to particular life events; and, of great importance, does the patient become uncooperative and begin to deny illness at the start of an episode? If the latter behavior occurs, patients are more likely to relapse since they will often not appear for appointments at the very time they most need the therapeutic intervention. In these cases, it is very important to develop relationships with family or other concerned individuals who have been educated about early signs of relapse and who will report early symptoms to the therapist.

Most previous studies on the decompensation process were carried out by gifted clinicians who considered individual cases.

Their usual approach was a detailed case study in which information was gathered retrospectively from both patients and family members. Docherty et al. (1978), reviewing the literature on stages of onset of schizophrenic psychosis, were able to sift out specific phases or stages of decompensation based on case reports. They differentiated five stages, the first two stages being nonpsychotic.

A conclusion that can be drawn from these studies is that, for a great many schizophrenic patients who have been in a stable condition, there is a nonpsychotic prodromal phase prior to the development of severe psychotic symptomatology. It is important for the clinician to understand that this occurs, to be able to recognize these symptoms, to discuss them with the patient, to engage the family or others as allies who will report early symptoms to the therapist, and to be prepared to initiate prompt therapeutic measures to prevent the development of a full-blown relapse. It should be mentioned that we do not yet know whether it is an early stage in the development of a psychotic episode each time a patient develops nonpsychotic symptomatology. However, a cautious clinician would observe the patient more closely during these times, initiating more frequent therapeutic contacts and increasing medication if indicated.

INTERMITTENT MEDICATION FOR STABLE SCHIZOPHRENIC OUTPATIENTS

It is routine practice to treat schizophrenic patients in the community with maintenance neuroleptic medication on an indefinite basis. The efficacy of antipsychotic medication in helping to prevent relapse has been established. However, there is growing concern about the potential deleterious side effects. This section will describe the results of a pilot study of 19 patients in an alternative strategy that took them off maintenance medication, treating them with antipsychotic medication only when they showed early signs of relapse.

Prolonged administration of neuroleptic drugs often has serious untoward side effects for patients, especially the development of tardive dyskinesia. Chouinard et al. (1979) report that 30 percent of schizophrenic outpatients treated with neuroleptics had tardive dyskinesia. The APA Task Force (1980) reports a prevalence of 10 to 20 percent in patients exposed to neuroleptics for more than 1 year. It is generally accepted that the incidence of tardive dyskinesia increases the longer the individual is maintained on the medication.

Bleuler (1978), who followed 208 schizophrenic patients for an average of 22 years, recommends that drugs be used only when relapse threatens, and not on a maintenance basis. He believes that the need for long-term maintenance therapy with neuroleptics is much overrated. Interestingly, several prominent psychopharmacologists have supported this viewpoint (Gardos and Cole 1976; Baldessarini 1977). In the *Manual of Psychiatric Therapeutics*, Shader and Jackson (1975) state that "while there are no clear guidelines that dictate the discontinuation of antipsychotic medications, ambulatory patients who have attained a complete remission for about six months might reasonably be given a trial with no antipsychotic medication." It is their opinion that "if a patient's aftercare program provides for reasonably frequent visits, it should be possible for the physician to see whether a patient's clinical status is beginning to deteriorate. In most instances medication can be increased before frank relapse occurs." It should be pointed out that previous studies comparing drug and placebo in schizophrenic outpatients have not emphasized the use of intervention with known active antipsychotic medication to prevent relapse when prodromal symptoms first appear. Thus the study we will describe is a significant departure from previous studies (Herz et al. 1982).

Two small pilot studies were carried out sequentially, one we call Group A, the other Group B. Both were conducted at community mental health centers, where patients were referred to the study by staff members.

Procedure

To be included in the study, patients had to (1) be age 19 to 60; (2) meet DSM-II criteria for diagnosis of schizophrenia in Group A and DSM-III criteria for Group B, patients in both groups having had at least two hospitalizations for schizophrenic symptomatology; (3) be outpatients in remission with stable symptomatology and role functioning for at least 6 months; (4) be maintained on antipsychotic medication; and (5) have no evidence of organic brain syndrome, serious medical illness, or suicidal or assaultive behavior during the previous 2 years.

Patients were seen weekly in group therapy sessions. During the first four group sessions, patients were instructed about early signs of schizophrenic relapse and the usefulness of medication during the prodromal phase. The importance of awareness of life events that could precipitate relapse was also emphasized. The group leader, a psychiatrist, was responsible for medications and made himself available to participants, at least by phone, at all times. Family members were also involved and educated about issues relating to relapse and uses of medication.

Stage I "Washout Period." Openly, over an average of 8 weeks, medications were gradually reduced to zero. Any patients showing increased symptomatology or decreased role functioning during Stage I were restarted on their previous levels of medication. The aim of Stage I was to distinguish patients for whom the medication was actively controlling symptomatology from patients for whom the medication was only prophylactic, i.e., useful only when symptoms appeared, signaling a probable relapse.

Stage II. Those patients who successfully completed Stage I and for whom the medication was prophylactic were kept medication-free. If at a later time symptoms considered potentially prodromal to relapse occurred, medications were reinstituted and patients were seen or in telephone contact with the group leader at least three times a week. Once the patient was stable for 2 weeks, the medications were gradually discontinued again.

Measurements. At the time of the original interview with the patient, demographic data were collected, as well as details of illness history, social relations, and functioning during the past year.

At the end of each group therapy session, the group leader completed a Problem Appraisal Scale (PAS) and Global Assessment Scale (GAS) (Endicott et al. 1976) for each patient. Patients were also asked each week whether they had experienced any stressful life events.

Group Therapy. Group therapy has been shown to be efficacious in the treatment of chronic schizophrenic patients (O'Brien et al. 1972; Herz et al. 1974). The group had four purposes: patient education, monitoring of clinical status, supportive therapy, and encouraging patients to provide mutual support for each other.

Subjects

Only descriptions of patients' courses were recorded from Group A (N = 5). All reported demographic data and symptom ratings are from Group B (N = 14). The patients in Group B included seven men, and had a mean age of 43.5 years. Five were married; six widowed, divorced, or separated; and three had never married. Half of the group lived with another adult. Mean lifetime hospitalizations were 2.4. Only four were presently employed.

Mean baseline symptomatology on nonpsychotic PAS items was generally in the mild range. No patient was experiencing delusions or hallucinations. Examination of individual patient's ratings reveals that eight were considered mildly or moderately impaired in their relations with others and six were rated as mildly or moderately socially withdrawn, one markedly.

The mean GAS rating was 62.7 (range, 51–71). The interval from 51 to 60 is described as "moderate symptoms or generally functioning with some difficulty (e.g., few friends and flat affect . . .)." The range from 61 to 70 is described as "some mild symptoms or some difficulty in several areas of functioning, but generally functioning pretty well. . . ."

Results

Stage I "Washout." While medications were being reduced on the 19 patients, 5 (26 percent) showed increased symptoms, and one of these was hospitalized. All five were placed back on maintenance medication.

The patient who was hospitalized had separated from her common-law husband within 2 weeks after the beginning of Stage I. Her medications were gradually reduced without instability until the fifth week of Stage I, when, against advice, she abruptly discontinued medication. In the sixth week of Stage I, she began to experience difficulty getting along with others, increased anxiety and depression, and paranoia and loose associations. Because she refused to take medications on an outpatient basis, she was hospitalized to prevent further deterioration. In retrospect, it was a mistake to reduce medication while the patient was experiencing a severe life stress.

Increases in the levels of symptoms were not severe for the other patients. They all suffered decreased sleep. Anxiety and impaired social relations increased to mild or moderate. In one patient, depression and social withdrawal were marked. None demonstrated any psychotic symptoms. The mean duration of elevations in PAS ratings was 5 weeks (range, 1–11 weeks).

Stage II. Of the 19 patients, 14 completed Stage I successfully. Subsequently, one patient dropped out; he was asymptomatic, but asked to be placed back on medication because of his wife's anxiety about his being off medication. Group A patients were followed for 6 months. Group B patients were followed for a mean of over 8 months (range, 13–45 weeks). Examination of patients' monthly mean scores on PAS items and GAS ratings while off medication and in remission, compared with their baseline scores on medication, showed no differences. This confirms the observations of Hogarty and co-workers (1973) that medication is prophylactic for most stable schizophrenic outpatients. When these patients are taken off medication, they showed no change in symptoms or role functioning.

Of the 13 patients who were followed during Stage II, 5 had a stable course throughout, with no perceptible changes in symptoms. Three of these were followed for 6 months and 2 for 11 months. Five patients had one or two prodromal episodes, after which medications were discontinued again. Typical symptoms were sleep disturbances, agitation, anxiety, anger, social withdrawal, and impaired social relations. In two cases, there were prepsychotic symptoms, e.g., distrust of others. All symptoms were quickly reversed with medication. Episodes lasted a mean of 1.4 weeks. From the beginning of a prodromal episode, patients remained on a full dose of their medication for a mean of 5 weeks; then medication was reduced to zero in 2 weeks. The mean highest drug dose was 180 mg chlorpromazine equivalents (range, 80–320 mg).

One patient had three prodromal episodes. For her benefit, it was decided to continue maintenance medication. A second patient experienced a nonpsychotic hypomanic episode in the fifth week of Stage II. On further examination, this patient was rediagnosed as schizoaffective schizophrenia. She was placed on lithium and chlorpromazine for the remainder of the study.

One patient was hospitalized. Two months after medication had been discontinued, he started to become withdrawn, but refused to go back on medication. Over a period of 5 weeks, the GAS rating dropped 25 points. In the sixth week, he developed paranoid delusions. His condition continued to deteriorate, and he refused medication. He was hospitalized for 5 days and put on medication.

Table 2 Clinical Courses of Schizophrenic Outpatients

Course	Group A (N = 5)	Group B (N = 14)	Total (N = 19)
Stage I (drug washout)			
Entered	5	14	19
Terminated	1	4	5
Stage 2			
Entered	4	10	14
Dropped out	1	0	1
Continued on intermittent medication protocol	3	7	10
No increase in baseline symptoms	3	2	5
1 or 2 prodromal episodes	0	5	5
Discontinued from protocol	0	3	3
2 prodromal episodes, rediagnosed	0	1	1
3 prodromal episodes	0	1	1
Hospitalized	0	1	1

In summary, 19 patients entered Stage I, and 5 washed out. Of the 14 who entered Stage II, 5 had stable courses; 5 had one or two prodromal episodes that were treated with intermittent medications, which were discontinued after the patients remitted; 2 were placed back on maintenance medication; 1 had a relapse and then remained on maintenance medication; and 1 dropped out of the study.

Comparison of Stage I Washouts with Those Who Entered Stage II. When patients whose symptoms increased during medication reduction are compared with those who remained stable, one notes that the former were more likely to have never married (50 percent versus 10 percent). Of those washouts, 75 percent (versus 50 percent) had an onset of illness before they were 30 years old. Two of the washouts (versus none) were hospitalized during the past year. Although the numbers are not large enough to draw firm conclusions from PAS items, there was a tendency for those who washed out to have slightly higher baseline scores on withdrawal, anxiety, and impaired relations with others. The mean GAS rating of those who washed out was 59.3 versus 64.2—a small difference, although the scores of the washouts fall in a lower interval. The initial mean maintenance medication dose in chlorpromazine equivalents was 555 mg for the washouts and 250 mg for those entering Stage II. Except for the one Stage II relapse who had been on 690 mg, there was no overlap.

Life Events. Symptomatic deterioration during the washout stage was usually not associated with a stress. On the other hand, for those who survived the washout period and for whom medication could be considered prophylactic, a life event usually preceded the appearance of prodromal symptoms.

Conclusions

The results of this pilot study must be viewed with caution because of the small numbers of patients involved. What are some of the tentative implications of the results?

Among the population of patients who are maintained on medication as outpatients and are considered stable, there are at least two groups. The first group is controlled on the medication; that is, the medication is actively controlling psychotic symptomatology. As the medication is gradually withdrawn during a washout period, the symptomatology begins to reemerge. Obviously, these patients are not candidates for intermittent therapy and must be maintained on medication. It is possible that, in the future, some patients will become less vulnerable to medication withdrawal.

At present there is no way of predicting which of the stable patients are being controlled on the medication. Therefore, gradual reduction with careful monitoring is necessary. This gradual withdrawal or washout period is relatively safe. Only one patient had a relapse requiring hospitalization during this stage, and it was associated with a severe life stress. It is not known whether this patient would have relapsed if there had been no such stress.

A second group of patients who were stable on medication showed no ill effects during the withdrawal period. These patients manifested the same symptom level while off medication. It is postulated that maintenance medication is effective for these patients because it is present during periods of stress when patients are most vulnerable to decompensation. However, the alternative approach of introducing medication during a prodromal stage proved to be effective as well. Only one patient in this group relapsed and required rehospitalization. For the others who had prodromal episodes, the introduction of active medication for a period averaging 5 weeks prevented relapse from occurring. Their symptoms were never severe; there were no major ill effects on role functioning, and no major disruptions in their lives. Of course, we do not know whether some of these so-called prodromal episodes would have progressed to full relapse without treatment because medication was introduced when symptoms first appeared.

Only two patients relapsed and were rehospitalized during the entire study period. This relapse rate of 11 percent indicates that the procedure is relatively safe. This compares favorably with the estimate of G. E. Hogarty (personal communication) that 15 percent of stable patients maintained on medication will relapse within 1 year, and 68 percent of stable patients taken off maintenance medication will relapse within 1 year.

It is evident that patients who are not stable while on medication or who require high doses of maintenance medication should not be withdrawn from medication. It is preferable that patients have a significant other who is willing to cooperate with the psychiatrist. During the prodromal period, some patients lose insight about their illness, becoming uncooperative and not showing up for therapy sessions. At these times, the cooperation of a significant other may be crucial. Patients experiencing stressful life events should be monitored more closely. Patients are more vulnerable to psychotic decompensation at these times and may need medication and increased psychosocial support.

A problem in conducting this pilot study, compared with a controlled study using placebos, is that many patients and their families were fearful about the patients' being without medication when medications were openly discontinued. For years they had been told that medication was necessary, similar to the diabetic's need for insulin, and that going off medication would be dangerous. The analogy with insulin for diabetes is not wholly correct. When a diabetic patient goes off insulin, the patient shows immediate signs of metabolic dyscontrol. This holds true only for schizophrenic patients who are controlled on medication and begin to deteriorate as the medicine is reduced. For patients who are maintained and who show no ill effects when medication is withdrawn, a better analogy might be that the action of medication is similar to but not as effective as penicillin for rheumatic fever prophylaxis.

The results of this pilot study, which can be considered only tentative, do provide justification for the large-scale double-blind controlled research study that my colleagues and I are presently conducting. Based on our experience, we believe that clinicians may safely attempt drug withdrawal with an intermittent approach for stable schizophrenic outpatients in remission who are seen weekly and who have a cooperative significant other.

References

APA Task Force on Late Neurological Effects of Antipsychotic Drugs: Tardive dyskinesia: summary of a task force report of the American Psychiatric Association. Am J Psychiatry 137:1163–1172, 1980

Baldessarini RJ: Chemotherapy in Psychiatry. Cambridge, Harvard University Press, 1977

Bleuler ME: The long-term course of schizophrenic psychoses, in The Nature of Schizophrenia: New Approaches to Research and Treatment. Edited by Wynne L, Cromwell RL, Matthysse S. New York, John Wiley & Sons, 1978, p 631

Chouinard G, deMontigny C, Annable L: Tardive dyskinesia and antiparkinsonian medication. Am J Psychiatry 136:228–229, 1979

Ciompi L: The natural history of schizophrenia in the long-term. Br J Psychiatry 136:413–420, 1980

Docherty JP, Van Kammen DP, Siris SG, et al: Stages of onset of schizophrenic psychosis. Am J Psychiatry 135:420–426, 1978

Endicott J, Spitzer RL, Fleiss JL, et al: The Global Assessment Scale: a procedure for measuring overall severity of psychiatric disturbance. Arch Gen Psychiatry 33:766–771, 1976

Englehardt DM, Rosen B, Feldman J, et al: A 15 year followup of 646 schizophrenic outpatients. Schizophr Bull 8:493–503, 1982

Gardos G, Cole JO: Maintenance antipsychotic therapy: is the cure worse than the disease? Am J Psychiatry 133:32–36, 1976

Herz MI, Melville C: Relapse in schizophrenia. Am J Psychiatry 137:801–805, 1980

Herz MI, Spitzer RL, Gibbon M, et al: Individual versus group aftercare treatment. Am J Psychiatry 131:808–812, 1974

Herz MI, Szymanski HV, Simon JC, et al: Intermittent medication for stable schizophrenic outpatients: an alternative to maintenance medication. Am J Psychiatry 139:918–922, 1982

Hogarty GE, Goldberg C, the Collaborative Study Group: Drugs and sociotherapy in the aftercare of schizophrenic patients. Arch Gen Psychiatry 28:54–64, 1973

Huber G, Gross G, Schuttler R, et al: Longitudinal studies of schizophrenic patients. Schizophr Bull 6:592–605, 1980

O'Brien CP, Hamm KB, Ray BA, et al: Group vs individual psychotherapy with schizophrenics: a controlled outcome study. Arch Gen Psychiatry 27:474–478, 1972

Shader RI, Jackson AH: Approaches to schizophrenia, in Manual of Psychiatric Therapeutics: Practical Psychopharmacology and Psychiatry. Edited by Shader RI. Boston, Little, Brown and Co, 1975

Spitzer RL, Endicott J, Cohen GM: Psychiatric Status Schedule, 2nd ed. New York, New York State Psychiatric Institute, 1968

Spitzer RL, Endicott J, Robins E: Research Diagnostic Criteria (RDC) for a Selected Group of Functional Disorders, 2nd ed. New York, New York State Psychiatric Institute, 1975

5

Intermittent Pharmacotherapy of Schizophrenia

William T. Carpenter, Jr., M.D.
Douglas W. Heinrichs, M.D.

5

Intermittent Pharmacotherapy of Schizophrenia

An appreciation of risks associated with standard pharmacotherapeutic approaches to schizophrenia has resulted in a search for alternative strategies that can achieve significant drug reduction without substantially increasing the rate or severity of psychotic exacerbation. Prominent among these risks is tardive dyskinesia. There is also the nagging concern that neuroleptics may increase the deficit symptoms such as apathy, anhedonia, and cognitive narrowing in stable outpatients. Hypothetically, there is the additional possibility that substantial use of these drugs may undermine their antipsychotic efficacy. A portion of patients experience sufficiently unpleasant side effects to result in their noncompliance with medication. If strategies of drug reduction can reduce these effects, they may prove especially suitable for this subpopulation of patients.

The plausibility of achieving a meaningful decrease from current drug dosage standards is suggested by several observations. First, causal comparisons of the differing medication strategies used in other countries have failed to suggest an enhanced therapeutic effect associated with the generally higher doses used in the United States. Second, trials of antipsychotics at high doses have not proven superior to standard doses (Davis et al. 1978), nor have loading dose strategies proven superior to fixed dose (Kirkpatrick and Burnett 1982). Several drug reduction approaches are of current interest and are discussed in this text.

In low dose strategies, patients receive medicine continuously but at lower than conventional doses (see Chapters 1–3). In drug holiday strategies, medication is discontinued for limited periods at fixed intervals in stable patients (Caffey et al. 1964; Prien and Klett 1972; Prien et al. 1973; Carpenter et al. 1977; Kurucz and Fallon 1980).

In selected circumstances, non-neuroleptic drugs (e.g., lithium carbonate, antiseizure medication, antianxiety drugs) are utilized, reducing or eliminating the need for conventional antipsychotics (Donaldson et al. 1983). Even more speculative are strategies attempting to down-regulate dopamine receptors or utilization of beta-blocking drugs (Friedhoff and Alpert 1978). Another strategy involves intermittent pharmacotherapy aimed at intervention at the earliest signs of impending psychotic relapse in drug-free patients.

This discussion describes our experience with the last of these approaches. One would expect the clinical context for this or any of the other reduction strategies to require (1) continuity of care to enable early detection of relapse, (2) the integration of a clinical treatment team so that pharmacotherapeutic interventions can be closely integrated with psychosocial treatment approaches, and (3) the education of the clinical team about the circumstances dictating the initiation or increase of medication so that those clinicians optimally suited for continual monitoring are also well informed concerning pharmacotherapeutic requirements. Clinicians personally involved in the patients' longitudinal care should be available to facilitate patient cooperation and to enhance sensitive decision making concerning changes in pharmacologic strategy. These principles of clinical care may contrast with standard practice, but they seem to be the minimal reasonable requirements for the long-term treatment of schizophrenia regardless of the pharmacologic strategy pursued, including the conventional one (Heinrichs and Carpenter 1982).

METHOD OF STUDY

To evaluate the relative effectiveness and limitation of a strategy of early drug intervention contrasted to one of continuous antipsychotic drug use, we initiated an aftercare program for schizophrenic outpatients who are diagnosed schizophrenic and who meet Research Diagnostic Criteria for schizophrenia or schizoaffective illness (mainly the outpatients were diagnosed as being schizophrenic).

Patients are withdrawn from medication for a 28-day period and then randomly assigned either to continuous drug treatment using standard dose levels of 300 mg/day of chlorpromazine equivalents (clinician adjustment permitted), or to intermittent, targeted drug treatment. Changes in medication status are triggered by prodromal symptoms, suggesting an impending decompensation, that is, medication is increased in the continuous drug group and initiated in the targeted drug group. Following restabilization, patients are returned to their baseline medication status.

The principal aim of the targeted, early intervention strategy is to achieve therapeutic and prophylactic effects of antipsychotic drugs without continuous drug exposure. If successful, the targeted approach may be a generally acceptable alternative to continuous drug treatment. From a clinical perspective, it seems an especially cogent strategy for noncompliant patients whose resistance to continuous medication is based on dysphoric effects of the drugs. These patients may collaborate with a more targeted use of drugs since they are less likely to experience drug-induced subjective distress when drugs are received only during active psychotic processes. Furthermore, this strategy may help identify those patients who do not require long-term drug administration because they are not drug responsive or because their courses of illness are no longer comprised of relapse and positive symptom exacerbations.

As part of the aftercare program, clinical assessment of all patients at baseline and at 6-month intervals during 2 years of active treatment is accomplished by an independent rater not involved in the treatment.

RESULTS

Because this study is in its preliminary stage, the results will be presented discursively. An initial consideration is whether medication withdrawal is feasible in an outpatient schizophrenic population. Our experience is based on all admissions to the clinic, and patients were not selected as "good" candidates for drug withdrawal. We have found that about three-fourths of the cases can sustain an abrupt cessation of drugs for a 28 day period without signs of positive symptom decompensation. Abrupt cessation was chosen to enhance detection of covert dyskinesia (Carpenter et al. 1980). Of the first 101 patients entering the drug discontinuation phase of the study, 29 did manifest signs of clinical decompensation. Drug treatment was reinstituted in these cases, and 21 of the 29 patients reattained their clinical baseline status in an average of 3.3 weeks. More troublesome were 8 patients who required rehospitalization during relapse. If one assumes the severe relapse rate associated with drug withdrawal is approximately twice that of drug continuation, the abrupt drug discontinuation strategy resulted in four more cases than would have relapsed with hospitalization had drugs been continued. Not surprisingly, a few patients successfully completing the drug-free period refused to accept their subsequent random assignment to continuous drugs in view of their enhanced sense of well-being off medication. This is a potential risk of drug discontinuation strategies and is often seen in clinics in the form of noncompliance alluded to above.

Experience to date reveals a similar course of illness in the experimental group compared to the continuous drug group. Data recorded on the Outcome Scale (Hawk et al. 1975), Global Assessment Scales (Endicott et al. 1976), the Quality of Life scale (Heinrichs et al. in press), and the Brief Psychiatric Rating Scale (Overall and Gorham 1962) revealed no statistically significant differences in outcome at 24 months between 12 targeted and 24 continuous drug patients. Although not statistically significant, hospital readmissions appear to be substantially more frequent in the targeted drug approach. Utilization of hospital resources (average days in hospital) was similar, however, in the two groups, suggesting briefer hospital stays and the possibility of more rapid therapeutic responsivity in patients decompensating in the targeted group.

Finally, there were statistically significant differences in the expected direction concerning the extent of medication use. Patients in the intermittent, targeted drug group were on medication an average of 45 percent of the time over the 2 years, contrasted with 96 percent of the time for the continuous drug group. There was a comparable dissimilarity in the cumulative dose of medication during the two years.

As indicated, patients had not been selected for the study because they fit preconceived notions of who would be good candidates for the targeted drug approach. This allows an empirical search for predictors of successful cases and predictors of unsuccessful cases. In this regard, it is important to note that the targeted drug approach was employed successfully in over 80 percent of the patients randomized to this treatment. Two of the 12 patients could not be maintained for substantial periods of time off medication and averaged 98.5 percent of the time on drugs. These 2 patients had decidedly negative outcomes and were de facto continuous drug patients, although their data were considered within the group of their random assignment. Of 12 patients who proved suitable for the targeted drug strategy, 10 achieved a substantial reduction in days on medication (34 percent of the time on drugs) and tended to have a more favorable outcome than the group as a whole.

CLINICAL IMPLICATIONS

There already exists a considerable body of clinical experience with intermittent drug approaches that has been reviewed favorably from the perspective of the long-term European studies (Bleuler 1978; Huber et al. 1979; Ciompi, 1980). Experience in the preliminary phase of this controlled study affirms the feasibility of such a strategy in the majority of chronically and severely ill schizophrenic patients. The practicing clinician may do even better than our experience would suggest. In the first place, we may have more clinical disruptions associated with our practice of abrupt drug cessation than the clinician would find with gradual drug reduction. Secondly, we randomly assign all cases, whereas the prudent physician would use common sense criteria to discern those subjects likely to be the best candidates. Such criteria would likely include the rapidity of onset of psychosis in past episodes, frequency and severity of relapse, the degree of insight maintained early in relapse, and the strength of the patient's collaboration in treatment (see Chapter 4). After initial screening, those patients empirically determined not to be good candidates would become de facto continuous medication patients in ordinary clinical practice.

CLINICAL STRATEGY ASSOCIATED WITH THE TARGETED DRUG APPROACH

In general, the clinical management necessary to implement targeted medication with schizophrenic patients conforms to the same principles that provide for optimal comprehensive care of schizophrenic patients on continuous medication. However, a number of features of treatment are particularly salient for the patient involved in the targeted approach.

In the initial phases of treatment, it is especially important to develop a shared view of the illness among therapist, patient, and family members. Prompt targeted intervention is most likely to occur when there is a common framework for conceptualizing subtle changes in the patient's clinical state and for planning the appropriate intervention. We begin treatment with a series of six educational visits for the patient and family members that are conducted by the patient's primary therapist. In this setting, both patient and relatives are encouraged to describe their experience of the illness from their own perspectives. The therapist attempts to identify areas of confusion or misinformation and elicits questions from the participants. The therapist then provides relevant information as to the nature of schizophrenic psychopathology, theories of etiology, patterns of course and outcome, and rationale for various treatments. Specific attention is paid to the rationale for targeted drug intervention. It is stressed that the use of medication is not evidence of failure and that it is fully expected that almost all patients will require medication from time to time. It is stressed that the use of medication will be time limited, so that medications will once again be discontinued when the patient's condition is stabilized.

Considerable time is taken in these early sessions to focus on the pattern of prodromal symptoms that each patient has manifested in previous episodes. Patients and relatives often need considerable help in this effort because prodromals have often been overshadowed by the more dramatic symptoms of florid psychosis. By having patients and relatives carefully focus on the 2 or 3 weeks prior to florid illness, it is usually possible to reconstruct a set of subjective and behavioral changes that have preceded past psychotic episodes (Herz and Melville 1980). Some common prodromal symptoms that have been identified with our patients are transient hallucinations, increased suspiciousness, changes in sleep patterns, free-floating anxiety, various somatic complaints, impaired concentration and muddled thinking, periods of anger and/or depression, and social withdrawal. Once prodromal symptoms have been delineated, it is stressed that patient, family, and therapist have a shared responsibility to remain vigilant for the appearance of such symptoms in the future so that prompt reinstitution of medication can be implemented.

The ongoing monitoring of the patient's condition is most enhanced by regular visits so that most impending episodes can be detected in the early stage of relapse. Although continued weekly visits are a built-in feature of our research design, it is our impression that a number of patients internalize the strategy of early recognition of relapse so effectively that weekly visits may not be necessary after the first 3 to 6 months. Such insightful patients are able to recognize an impending relapse independently and contact the therapist for the initiation of treatment. There remain, however, a considerable number of patients who become aware of their impending relapse only when their clinician calls attention to it. Unless other people in the patient's environment can perform this function, such patients may require frequent visits over an indefinite period. Once the patient is well known to the therapist, however, these visits can often be quite brief.

In either case, 24-hour availability of the clinical staff is critical. The need for prompt action when prodromal symptoms appear is stressed with patients and their families. It is necessary, therefore, that treatment be initiated as quickly as possible when such symptoms are recognized. We provide an emergency phone number at which patients and families can reach a member of the clinical team 24 hours a day, 7 days a week. Appropriate use of this service requires considerable reeducation of patients and their families. For example, there is a reluctance to disturb clinicians after hours for subtle prodromal changes. As a consequence, we have had to stress our preference for dealing with prodromal changes on a Saturday evening rather than a full-blown relapse Monday morning.

Either spontaneously or in response to observations by the therapist, the majority of our patients can recognize they are getting sick in the early phases of relapse. A patient's capacity for this early insight appears to be an important variable in predicting the efficacy of the targeted intervention strategy. When such insight is present, the majority of relapses can be treated on an outpatient basis with rapid reinstitution of medication. In the absence of this minimum insight, pharmacotherapy is delayed and hospitalization is likely. Given the importance of this variable, we are attempting to foster insight in those patients who have not manifested it during previous decompensations. Many such patients learn from their previous failure to recognize early relapse. In some patients, this has taken the form of realization that the failure to use medication in certain circumstances has consistently led to hospitalization. Based on this, some patients will cooperate in the targeted drug strategy even if they themselves are not convinced that their symptoms represent a recurrence of illness. This seems especially likely to occur when they have developed a trusting relationship with their primary clinician. It has been useful in a number of cases to involve a trusted companion of the patient (e.g., a relative or employer). In such cases, the patient and therapist have agreed to contact this person for an objective assessment of the patient's functioning and behavior at times when the therapist suspects a relapse but the patient is unconvinced. For some patients, the objective confirmation of deterioration in their behavior by this person results in their compliance with medication intervention. We have also found a few patients who, despite the explanation given at the beginning of treatment, deny the onset of deterioration because they believe that the resumption of medication indicates a failure of the targeted strategy and that they will then be required to stay on medication indefinitely. In these instances, we emphasize that medication is being prescribed on a time-limited basis, and that periodic symptom exacerbations are expected and do not constitute a failure of treatment.

An unanticipated challenge in the management of patients using the targeted drug strategy is helping them cope with the brightening and increased activation that is often experienced in the drug-free state. A considerable number of patients feel more energized, more interested in interacting with others, and more motivated to increase their functional level when drug free. Unfortunately, the increased drive is not accompanied by an increase in social and instrumental skills, so that there is a tendency for some patients to rush headlong into situations for which they are poorly equipped. Resulting stress and failure can be both demoralizing to the patient and a precipitant to psychotic relapse. This is often made worse by the syndrome of "making up for lost time." As patients become more energized, they frequently become acutely aware of the undeveloped potential resulting from their illness. They see peers who have progressed further and accomplished more, and they frequently feel a strong urgency to catch up. As a result, they conceive overly ambitious plans that are socially or occupationally unrealistic. To counter this, we have focused attention on teaching patients the importance of gradual progress in functioning and a careful monitoring of their stress level. Also important in this regard is helping patients develop specific skills needed to carry out their plans.

The targeted drug strategy encourages a high level of participation by patients in their own treatment. They are urged to be sensitive to the occurrence of prodromal symptoms, to seek the opinions of family members and other important persons in their lives, and to contact the therapist promptly. Reflecting on this process has proved a useful beginning for a number of patients in counteracting the passivity so intrinsic to the schizophrenic illness. Successful use of this strategy during therapy can instill a sense of mastery in many patients that can sometimes be generalized to other facets of their life. A number of our patients have shown increased self-esteem as they assume an active role in controlling their illness.

The implementation of the targeted drug strategy requires comprehensive attention to signs and symptoms, pharmacologic considerations, level of patient insight, features of the patient's social environment, and factors influencing the level of stress experienced by the patient. As a result, pharmacologic decisions cannot be made in a vacuum. There needs to be full collaboration between the psychosocial treatment provided and decisions about medication.

In our clinic and most other settings this requirement is complicated by the fact that various aspects of the patient's treatment are handled by separate individuals. The ongoing weekly therapeutic contact with the patient in our project is provided by either a psychiatric social worker or a master's level psychologist. When the therapist detects a change in clinical state that may require the initiation of medication, the therapist and patient together meet with the psychiatrist. The resultant three-way discussion has proven an effective and expedient format in which the psychiatrist can become generously informed about the psychosocial context of the patient's symptomatic change in a relatively brief period of time. The resultant decision about medication is thus in response to a comprehensive view of the patient's needs. Such interdisciplinary exchange can only proceed smoothly when there is a shared model of the illness. A broad medical model that takes into account biologic, psychologic, and social dimensions of illness is ideal in this regard (Engle 1977; Strauss and Carpenter 1981).

CONCLUSIONS

We have described our preliminary experience with one alternative to standard pharmacotherapy in schizophrenic aftercare. This intermittent, targeted strategy attempts to maintain patients on a drug-free status, with careful attention paid to detecting early clinical changes suggestive of impending psychotic relapse. Pharmacotherapy is then quickly initiated but continues only until the patient is restabilized. Our experience to date suggests that such an approach leads to a significant decrease in medication exposure without compromising the clinical course compared to traditional continuous medication. A number of the clinical management issues germane to this strategy have been discussed.

References

Bleuler M: The Schizophrenic Disorders: Long-Term Patient and Family Studies. Translated by Clemens SM. New Haven, Yale University Press, 1978

Caffey EM Jr, Diamond LS, Frank TD, et al: Discontinuation or reduction of chemotherapy in chronic schizophrenics. J Chronic Dis 17:347–358, 1964

Carpenter WT, McGlashan TH, Strauss JS: The treatment of acute schizophrenia without drugs: an investigation of some current assumptions. Am J Psychiatry 134:14–20, 1977

Carpenter WT, Rey AC, Stephens JH: Covert dyskinesia in ambulatory schizophrenia. Lancet 2:212–213, 1980

Ciompi L: The natural history of schizophrenia in the long-term. Br J Psychiatry 136:413–420, 1980

Davis JM, Erickson S, Dekirmenjian H: Plasma levels of antipsychotic drugs and clinical response, in Psychopharmacology: A Generation of Progress. Edited by Lipton MA, DiMascio AL, Killam KF. New York, Raven Press, 1978

Donaldson SR, Gelenberg AJ, Baldessarini RJ: The pharmacologic treatment of schizophrenia: a progress report. Schizophr Bull 9:504–527, 1983

Endicott J, Spitzer RL, Fleiss JL, et al: The Global Assessment Scale: a procedure for measuring overall severity of psychiatric disturbance. Arch Gen Psychiatry 33:766–771, 1976

Engel GL: The need for a new medical model: a challenge for biomedicine. Science 196:129–136, 1977

Friedhoff AJ, Alpert M: Receptor sensitivity modification as a potential treatment, in Psychopharmacology: A Generation of Progress. Edited by Lipton MA, DiMascio A, Killam KF. New York, Raven Press, 1978

Hawk AB, Carpenter WT, Strauss JS: Diagnostic criteria and five-year outcome in schizophrenia. Arch Gen Psychiatry 32:343–347, 1975

Heinrichs DW, Carpenter WT: The psychotherapy of the schizophrenic disorders, in Psychiatry 1982: The American Psychiatric Association Annual Review. Edited by Grinspoon L. Washington DC, American Psychiatric Press, 1982

Heinrichs DW, Carpenter WT, Hanlon TE: The Quality of Life Scale: an instrument for rating the schizophrenic deficit syndrome. Schizophr Bull (in press)

Herz MI, Melville C: Relapse in schizophrenia. Am J Psychiatry 137:801–805, 1980

Huber G, Gross G, Scheuttler R: Schizophrenia, eine Verlaufs und Sozialpsychiatriatrische Langzeitstudie. Berlin, Springer, 1979

Kirkpatrick B, Burnett G: Observations on neuroleptic use in acutely psychotic patients. J Clin Psychopharmacol 2:205–207, 1982

Kurucz J, Fallon MS: Dose reduction and discontinuation of antipsychotic medication. Hosp Community Psychiatry 31:117–119, 1980

Overall JE, Gorham DR: The Brief Psychiatric Rating Scale. Psychol Rep 10:799–812, 1962

Prien RF, Klett CJ: An appraisal of the long-term use of tranquilizing medication with hospitalized chronic schizophrenics: a review of the drug discontinuation literature. Schizophr Bull 5:64–73, 1972

Prien RF, Gilis RD, Caffey EM: Intermittent pharmacotherapy in chronic schizophrenia. Hosp Community Psychiatry 24:317–322, 1973

Strauss JS, Carpenter WT: Schizophrenia. New York, Plenum, 1981

6

Discussion: Alternative Drug Treatment Strategies in Schizophrenia

Nina R. Schooler, Ph.D.

6

Discussion: Alternative Drug Treatment Strategies in Schizophrenia

This monograph includes much of the recent work on drug treatment strategies in schizophrenia. The focus of this work is on long-term maintenance treatment of schizophrenic patients. The goal of each of these studies is to minimize the amount of antipsychotic drug that patients are exposed to, thereby minimizing the risk and negative consequences of neuroleptics (which are assumed to be dose related), while maximizing the benefits of medication. This goal has obvious immediate and direct clinical applicability to large numbers of schizophrenic patients who are and who will be maintained on medication for extended periods of time.

Had a collection of papers on drug treatment strategies been assembled 10 or 15 years ago, the focus would have been quite different. The following studies might have been included: (1) a comparison of standard dose with high dose chlorpromazine in chronic hospitalized patients (Prien and Cole 1968); (2) a comparison of a fixed length drug holiday with continued treatment in chronic inpatients (Caffey et al. 1964); (3) comparison of rapid neuroleptization (high dose) with standard dose in acutely exacerbated newly hospitalized patients (Donlon et al. 1979).

The earlier literature on drug treatment strategies was far more concerned with the exploration of the high end of the relationship between dose and response. Further, these earlier studies were more likely to be conducted in hospital rather than community settings. They reflected the clinical concerns of their time: (1) the use of high doses to deal with patients and symptoms unresponsive to more conventional dosage in order to enable long-stay patients to be discharged; (2) the use of fixed length drug holidays and other manipulations of medication administration schedules in order to make more efficient use of nursing time while ensuring continued medication; and (3) the need for rapid symptomatic control of patients who returned to the hospital through the revolving door. The studies of high dosage reflected an assumption of a linear effect of neuroleptics on schizophrenic symptomatology. If 500 mg of chlorpromazine reduced symptoms in some patients by a certain amount, then a doubling of the dose should increase both the proportion of patients benefited and the magnitude of the symptom reduction. These studies reflect the optimism generated by the early promise of antipsychotic drugs. Two conclusions would have been drawn from this hypothetical anthology. The first is that increasing dosage among long-stay chronic patients or among acutely exacerbated patients did not make much difference. The second is that a certain amount of tinkering with timing of drug administration, including some hiatuses of several days or weeks, could be tolerated by many patients without disrupting their symptomatic equilibrium.

The current studies on reduced dosage treatment reflect concerns of more than 20 years of experience in the use of antipsychotic drugs. Prominent among these concerns is the risk of tardive dyskinesia (TD). The association of TD with neuroleptic drug exposure suggests that risk of TD is dosage dependent and that higher cumulative dose will be associated with greater risk of developing TD. It might be noted that this hypothesis of a linear relationship between cumulative dose and TD is very similar to the hypothesis of a linear relationship between dose and symptomatic response cited above. A second clinical concern focuses on the troublesome presence of residual "negative" symptoms in patients receiving antipsychotic drugs. Are these symptoms side effects caused by the drugs or characteristics and symptoms of the illness that are unresponsive to drug treatment? The earlier high dose studies were predicated, in part, on the hypothesis that the presence of symptoms meant that more medication was needed; the current studies hypothesize that less medication might be better. Finally, studies of dosage reduction may test a hypothesis of the mechanism of antipsychotic drug action; that the action of antipsychotics is not dopamine blockade per se but that neuroleptics function to trigger a series of responses in the dopaminergic system that may restore homeostasis at a more appropriate level (Friedhoff 1983).

The use of any drug treatment strategy depends in part on assumptions made regarding the nature of the illness being treated. The use of *continuous antipsychotic medication* at standard doses follows from one of two assumptions: either that the symptoms being treated are continuously present and are being kept under control by the medication, or that continuous medication may prevent the unpredictable reemergence of symptoms. A *reduced dosage* strategy accepts both the maintenance and prophylactic premises of continuous antipsychotic drug treatment but attempts to achieve that goal while minimizing the exposure to medication. This model assumes further that the presence of a continuous low dosage of medication serves to cushion the severity of symptom exacerbation when it does occur, and to enhance the speed of response to added medication when symptoms appear. A *drug holiday* approach also assumes both the maintenance and prophylactic benefits of continuous drug treatment but attempts to achieve them through the imposition of a fixed schedule of alternating medication and medication-free intervals. Determination of such schedules is based on general clinical and/or research experience rather than on clinical observation of individual patients. A *targeted medication* strategy assumes that medication is not continuously required to suppress psychotic symptoms in many patients and that medication will prevent or delay the emergence of symptoms if administered early during an exacerbation. This strategy depends on the early identification of prodromal symptoms to determine the timing of intervention with medication to treat the symptoms and to prevent a full relapse.

Once clinical stability is reestablished, medication is again discontinued.

The assumptions underlying the expectation of efficacy for these treatment strategies probably hold true for subpopulations of the patients treated and studied. How common each of these subgroups is and how to determine which strategy is more appropriate for which patient remain important questions for the researcher and, particularly, for the clinician.

With the exception of the study conducted by Rifkin and Kane (Chapter 2), all the other investigators are providing us with early glimpses into ongoing work. Although the final results of the studies are not yet known, there are several methodological questions that can be kept in mind for future scrutiny of study results. Some of these questions and an indication of how they might influence study results follow.

What was the dosage of medication that patients were receiving when they entered the study? In drug discontinuation studies with placebo substitution, patients who had received higher dosage of drug were more likely to relapse when placed on placebo than those who had received lower dosage (Prien et al. 1971). This factor is clearly applicable to the intermittent or targeted treatment studies, and might be applicable to the low dose strategies as well. Populations with lower starting doses would be less likely to show differences between treatment groups. Specifically, patients whose starting dosages were relatively low would be more successfully treated with either a targeted or low dose approach.

What was the length of time since the last episode of acute symptom exacerbation? Hogarty and Ulrich (1977) show that there is a declining risk of relapse following hospital discharge. The longer patients have been asymptomatic or stable, the more likely they are to remain that way.

What was the actual dosage employed in a low dose study? Rifkin and Kane (Chapter 2), using a 90 percent dosage reduction, reported significant differences in relapses, whereas Marder et al. (Chapter 3), using an 80 percent reduction, reported no difference.

What measure of outcome was used? If "success" of a given strategy is measured by relapse, we may come to a different set of conclusions than if success is measured by cumulative dosage received, family perception of burden, an assessment of the patient's satisfaction, or other aspects of quality of life.

What was the timing of outcome assessments? The problems in interpretation caused by multiple outcome measures are further increased by the differences that are a function of multiple assessments over time and the changes in a patient over time. In clinical management, a longitudinal perspective on a patient's condition is needed, and integration of this information about change is one of the functions of a good clinician. In research assessment, methods for integrating data over time are not well developed, so that we tend to rely on multiple cross-sectional "snap shots." This problem is highlighted when the goal of the research is to assess strategies longitudinally. It is not clear how the issue of longitudinal assessment would affect interpretation of results from the kinds of studies described.

Finally, drawing on the data presented regarding each of the reduced dosage strategies, on the concerns expressed by the authors and their convictions (some even supported by data), and on the methodological issues that have been identified as influencing outcome, it is possible to offer the clinician some guidance for management of individual schizophrenic patients in the community.

If the patient is schizophrenic according to current diagnostic criteria, then either an intermittent or reduced dosage treatment strategy may be in order.

Because none of the studies described above provides a direct comparison of the two strategies, a decision between them cannot be based on research findings. The distinction between the two treatments is not as pronounced in a clinician's hands as it must be in the researcher's, however, because the clinician's route to no medication probably involves dosage reduction along the way. Therefore, the clinician can stop at a given low dosage if that seems indicated.

As has been noted in several of the earlier chapters, the longer the time since an episode the lower the risk of relapse. Thus the length of the patient's clinical stability is an important factor to consider. In all the studies, at least several months of stability are prerequisite. One might expect that patients who have been in treatment for a long time might benefit from dose reduction or monitored discontinuation.

What dose is the patient currently receiving? If the patient's current dose is relatively high, it may reflect either the patient's current need or simply that the dose has not been changed from an earlier time.

If the patient shows symptoms that may be indicative of extrapyramidal side effects, these might respond to dosage reduction or discontinuation.

An environment that provides for monitoring—by the family, by the patient, or by the clinical support system—is an important prerequisite to a treatment that may increase the risk of relapse and the degree of clinical instability.

A review of the issues should place the clinician and the patient in a good position to decide whether to try dose reduction in an effort to obtain the possible benefits of reduced risk of TD and of improved psychological well-being without incurring substantial increased risk of relapse.

References

Caffey EM, Diamond LS, Frank TV, et al: Discontinuation or reduction of chemotherapy in chronic schizophrenia. J Chronic Dis 17:347–358, 1964

Donlon P, Hopkin J, Tupin J: Overview: efficacy and safety of the rapid neuroleptization method with injectible haloperidol. Am J Psychiatry 130:273–278, 1979

Friedhoff AJ: A strategy for developing novel drugs for the treatment of schizophrenia. Schizophr Bull 9:555–562, 1983

Hogarty GE, Ulrich RF: Temporal effects of drug and placebo in delaying relapse of schizophrenic patients. Arch Gen Psychiatry 34:297–301, 1977

Prien RF, Cole JO: High dose chlorpromazine therapy in chronic schizophrenia. Arch Gen Psychiatry 18:482–495, 1968

Prien RF, Levin J, Switalskin RW: Discontinuation of chemotherapy for chronic schizophrenia. Hosp Community Psychiatry 22:4–7, 1971